Water Lily Vase, 1895
By Emile Galle
Gift of Dr. and Mrs. J. Brian Eby

HOUSTON

Fine Arts

COOKBOOK

Edited by
Virginia T. Elverson

UNIVERSITY OF TEXAS PRESS
AUSTIN

LIBRARY OF CONGRESS
CATALOGING IN PUBLICATION DATA

Main entry under title:
Houston fine arts cookbook.
   Includes index.
   1. Cookery, American—Texas.   2. Cookery,
International.   I. Elverson, Virginia T.
TX715.H837   1983   641.5   83-10466
ISBN 0-292-73024-1

FOREWORD

Nature has long been the inspiration for artists. So it is appropriate that nature is the inspiration for the organization of this cookbook from The Museum of Fine Arts, Houston. Along with over 300 delectable recipes arranged in seasonal menus are illustrations of the magnificent changing views of the museum gardens and some of the masterpieces from the museum collection.

My sincere thanks go to Virginia Elverson and Susie Morris for making this cookbook a reality and to the many friends of the museum who spent a great deal of time collecting and testing the recipes in the *Houston Fine Arts Cookbook*.

PETER C. MARZIO
Director
The Museum of Fine Arts, Houston

CONTENTS

CONTENTS

Flour is measured, unsifted, in a metal, dry measure and leveled with a straight edge unless recipe calls for flour sifted before measuring. Flour is meant to be all-purpose flour unless otherwise specified.

Sugar is measured in the same way as flour and is meant to be granulated sugar unless otherwise specified.

Brown sugar is measured after being packed in the measure.

Eggs are large, Grade AA, and should measure about 5 eggs to an 8-ounce cup.

Butter is measured in tablespoons or ounces and is meant to be unsalted butter.

Zest is the oily, surface part of citrus fruits without the white pith.

Rind is the zest plus the pith of citrus fruits.

When fine food is beautifully prepared and presented, it can be a work of art that nourishes the emotional as well as the physical senses. The Museum of Fine Arts of Houston implemented this philosophy in 1974 when the Museum Restaurant opened, providing gallery guests with fine food to enhance the visual art experience. Gardens with continually changing displays of seasonal flowers and bulbs add to the pleasure of dining in this artistic environment.

The integration of art, food, and garden setting has provided the inspiration for the museum's "art cookbook." Concern for the total artistic experience is expressed in the seasonal organization of the menus, which are enhanced by color illustrations of relevant works of art from the museum's collection. Photographs of the gardens in various seasons are interspersed among the menus of that season. These illustrate the point that a well-planned meal, like a well-planned garden, always includes a harmonious balance of color and texture. Appropriate wines are suggested and introductory material for several menus in each season explains the significance of the occasion.

Because Texas has a unique history created by widely diverse ethnic groups, any cookbook made up of a collection of recipes should reflect these national cuisines. The French claimed Texas in the late seventeenth century but left no lasting culinary impact. No settlement of any consequence was established, but, indeed, had there been, the harsh reality of life in this part of the New World would certainly have not been conducive to elegant dining. Spanish domination, which lasted until 1820, introduced beef cattle and domestic animals, olive oil and wine, and many traditional Spanish seasonings, such as oregano and saffron. Though these additions to the *cocina* were confined largely to the string of Spanish Roman Catholic missions that stretched across Texas, they were combined by necessity with the Indian fare of corn, game, and indigenous herbs. The beginning of "Tex-Mex" food, which has gained such national popularity with today's gastronomic pioneers, was firmly established. Are there any Texans worth their chili powder who don't suffer withdrawal pangs when separated for any length of time from their favorite Mexican dishes? Indeed, there are those *tejanos* whose first stop on the way home from the airport is the nearest Tex-Mex restaurant serving tacos, guacamole, and chili con queso.

After 1821, when Mexico seized control of Texas, food habits remained much the same as under the previous Spanish rule. Texas declared and won independence in 1836 and, until joining the Union in 1845, the Lone Star banner flew proudly over the Republic. During the periods of both Mexican and Republican governments, settlement by immigrants from the United States as well as from Europe was encouraged by the ruling powers. Lured by the vast amounts of public land available and by glowing reports of verdant meadows, sparkling creeks, and an abundance of wild nuts, fruits, and game of all varieties, they came. From the Southern states came adventurers, fortune hunters, and planters with slaves and household possessions. With the latter came the culinary tastes and habits of gracious Southern dining, which reflected an English ancestry. In addition came greens, black-eyed peas, okra, yams, and other so-called soul food, which had its origins in the slave quarters of large plantations.

It was also during this period that numbers of German and mid-European immigrants moved to the state, spreading their language, culture, and cuisine throughout central Texas and west to San Antonio, New Braunfels, and Fredericksburg. Sausage, cabbage, kohlrabi, sweet wines and beer, kolaches, strudels, and dozens of similar ethnic dishes still dominate tables in those areas. Each fall Wurstfests and Oktoberfests remind us of these ethnic contributions to the Texas culinary melting pot.

Throughout the periods of the Republic, the Confederacy, and on into statehood, Texas continued to absorb settlers from all countries. Using local ingredients, these families adapted, modified, and refined their traditional recipes until the taste of the resulting dish met the high standards of nostalgic memories of the past.

The twentieth century has seen an unprecedented number of ethnic groups assimilated into this rich cultural broth. In Houston's Chinatown one can find a noodle factory, bean sprout greenhouse, dried lotus buds, fermented black beans, and hundreds of ingredients necessary to prepare the fine cuisine of China. Members of the Greek Orthodox Cathedral—the largest in the South—present a three-day Greek Festival each October, during which time thousands of visitors sample typical Greek fare while sipping Ouzo and Retsina. Hellenic import shops in the area stock Calymata olives, Kasseri and Feta cheeses, tahini, and chickpeas—all essential to Greek dishes. The Blessing of the Fleet is an event that officially opens shrimping season each April along the Texas Gulf Coast. During the past few years great numbers of Vietnamese have joined the forces bringing back the briny harvest, and shops in the area stock essential ingredients for dishes that are familiar to the Indo-Chinese population. Cuban markets and cafés; Indian suppliers of Bombay duck, ghee, pappadums, and tamarind paste; Nigerian food shops with palm oil, coconut products, and plantains all grow and prosper, side-by-side, in twentieth-century Houston. Finally, ethnic influences on our cuisine have come full circle back to the French, who own and operate some of the finest bakeries, patisseries, and restaurants in our area.

To complete the total artistic palette—or palate, if you will—these culinary colors, shadings, shapes, and forms have been contrasted and combined to create menus that epitomize art in dining, Texas style.

Daffodils in South Garden

Spring Menus

Meeting of Solomon and the Queen of Sheba, *ca. 1470*
Tempera on panel, Ferrarese School
Edith A. and Percy S. Straus Collection

for Six

∗ Chilled Avocado Soup

∗ Polish Veal Roast with Caviar Sauce

∗ Rice Soubise

Steamed Green Beans Dressed with Butter

∗ Salad of Asparagus and Mushrooms Vinaigrette

∗ Lemon Cup

Sparkling Dry White Wine, Well Chilled

Pull out all the stops for this one. Ask one other, interesting couple to keep the atmosphere lighthearted. Polish the silver, add candlelight and plenty of fresh flowers—to let the boss know that he or she is "special." Soup and dessert can be prepared in the morning; soubise can be assembled and oven-ready. The roast may be cooked up to the point of adding caviar and finished just before serving. Fresh fruit may be added to the lemon cup for additional color and flavor contrast. It will be a great party—have fun!

Chilled Avocado Soup

SERVES 6 TO 8

2   large avocados
3½ cups homemade vegetable stock (see p. 221) or 3½ cups water with 1 teaspoon instant vegetable bouillon
½   cup plain yogurt
2   tablespoons lemon juice
½   teaspoon salt (omit if using salted or instant stock)
¼   teaspoon ground white pepper
8   drops Tabasco sauce
Chopped fresh dill or chives for garnish
Lime slices for garnish

Purée avocados in blender or processor. Add remaining ingredients except garnishes. Blend until smooth. Taste to adjust seasonings. Chill 2–3 hours or until well chilled. Serve with sprinkling of dill or chives and slice of lime.

Polish Veal Roast with Caviar Sauce

SERVES 6

2   tablespoons lard or vegetable shortening
4   pounds boned veal rump roast or leg
½   teaspoon salt
½   pound bacon, thinly sliced and blanched
4   carrots, chopped (about 1½ cups)
3   ribs celery, chopped (about ⅔ cup)
2   large onions, chopped (about 1½ cups)
3   ounces dry red wine
¾   cup chicken broth (see p. 221)
1   teaspoon whole black peppercorns
2   bay leaves, crumbled
Beurre manie (equal parts butter and flour, worked to smooth paste)
1   teaspoon butter
Juice of 1 lemon
3 to 4 ounces caviar (do not use caviar with color added)

Preheat oven to 325°.

Melt lard in large heavy saucepan. Heat until very hot. Brown all sides of roast. Remove roast. Salt meat lightly.

Line casserole (approximately size of roast) with bacon slices. Place chopped vegetables on bacon. Place roast on top of vegetables.

Drain fat from pan; deglaze pan with red wine and chicken broth. Pour on top of roast. Sprinkle peppercorns and bay leaves over roast. Cover. Bake 1½ hours.

When done, remove roast from casserole. Strain remaining juices through fine sieve, forcing chopped vegetables through sieve. Return mixture to stove. Add beurre manie, stirring constantly until as thick as light cream. Heat to boil.

Remove from heat. Add butter and lemon juice. Gently stir caviar into sauce, which should be thickness of heavy cream. Serve caviar sauce with sliced roast.

Rice Soubise

SERVES 6

3 cups water
1½ teaspoons salt, divided
¾ cup uncooked brown rice
6 tablespoons butter
6 to 8 large onions, quartered and sliced
    (about 6 cups)
⅓ cup half-and-half or whipping cream
⅓ cup freshly grated Parmesan cheese

Preheat oven to 350°.
Boil water with 1 teaspoon salt. Drop rice in water; boil, uncovered, 8 minutes. Drain rice. Set aside.
Melt butter in 2-quart glass casserole. Stir in onions and ½ teaspoon salt. Add rice. Cover and bake 1½ hours or until onions are tender. Stir in cream and Parmesan cheese. Place under broiler to brown.

Salad of Asparagus and Mushrooms Vinaigrette

SERVES 6

1½ pounds asparagus, washed and trimmed
1½ cups sliced fresh mushrooms
Vinaigrette (see p. 225) with 1 teaspoon
    dried tarragon added
Lettuce for garnish

Blanch asparagus 5 minutes or until tender crisp. Refresh in cold water. Place asparagus and mushrooms in shallow dish. Add vinaigrette. Refrigerate several hours or overnight. Serve on lettuce-lined plates.

Lemon Cup

SERVES 6

1 lemon, juice and zest
⅔ cup sugar, divided
2 tablespoons butter
3 eggs, separated
1 tablespoon flour
½ cup milk

Preheat oven to 325°.
Remove lemon zest with vegetable peeler. Do not include any of white pith. Process zest in processor or blender with ⅓ cup sugar until finely chopped. Cream mixture with butter until light and fluffy. Beat in egg yolks; blend in flour. Add lemon juice; mix thoroughly. Beat in milk.
In separate bowl beat egg whites until stiff. Continue to beat and add remaining sugar. Immediately fold into batter. Pour into lightly buttered 1-quart baking dish or 6 individual dishes. Bake 30 minutes. When cool, invert onto serving dish.

SUNDAY LUNCH FOR WEEKEND GUESTS

for Six

* Crab Madrilène
* Flank Steak
* Potatoes Gratiné with Mushrooms
* Spinach Salad
* Chocolate Mousse
  Chilled Dry Rosé

The Promenade, 1894
Oil painting by Edouard Vuillard
Blaffer Collection

Crab Madrilène

2 13-ounce cans consommé Madrilène
4 tablespoons dry sherry
½ cup Dijon mustard
6 scallions, including tops, finely chopped
1½ cups mayonnaise (see p. 223)
1 pound fresh lump crab meat
1 bunch watercress for garnish

Combine Madrilène and sherry in large shallow pan with liquid not more than ½ inch thick. Chill overnight until firm.

Add mustard and scallions to mayonnaise; mix well. Refrigerate overnight.

Chill 6 soup or shallow glass bowls. Using spoon or fork, chop Madrilène. Place in bowls. Top with crab. Cover with tablespoon of sauce. Garnish with watercress.

To serve as first course, salad, or luncheon entrée: Chill plates. Cut Madrilène into squares and place on watercress. Top with crab and sauce.

Flank Steak

SERVES 6

6 tablespoons butter
½ cup sesame seeds
2 cups coffee
½ cup soy sauce
2 onions, sliced
4 to 5 pounds flank steak
Fresh mushrooms, sliced and sautéed in butter (optional)

Lightly brown sesame seeds in butter. Combine with coffee, soy sauce, and onions. Marinate steak in mixture 1 day at room temperature.

Remove steak from marinade. Broil to desired doneness (5 minutes on each side for medium rare). Slice thinly on diagonal. Serve immediately.

Strain sesame seeds and sliced onions from marinade. Heat with mushrooms. Serve as optional garnish.

Potatoes Gratiné with Mushrooms

SERVES 6

Butter
1 cup heavy cream
¼ cup milk
1 clove garlic, finely chopped
½ teaspoon marjoram
¼ teaspoon ground white pepper
½ teaspoon salt
½ pound mushrooms, thinly sliced
1 pound potatoes, parboiled 10 minutes, peeled and very thinly sliced
¼ to ½ cup freshly grated Appenzell or Gruyère cheese

Preheat oven to 350°.
Generously butter shallow 1½- to 2-quart baking dish.
Combine cream, milk, garlic, and spices in large bowl. Add mushrooms and potatoes. Stir with wooden spoon until all slices are thoroughly coated. Pour into baking dish. Sprinkle top with grated cheese. Bake until potatoes are tender and top is golden brown (about 1¼ hours). Serve immediately.

Spinach Salad

SERVES 6

1 pound spinach
¾ pound bacon
2 hard-boiled eggs, finely chopped, for garnish

Dressing:
2 tablespoons bacon drippings
½ cup red wine vinegar
2 tablespoons tarragon vinegar
2 cloves garlic, pressed
⅔ cup salad oil
1 teaspoon Worcestershire sauce
1 teaspoon salt
½ teaspoon ground pepper

Wash, clean, and dry spinach; refrigerate. Cook bacon until crisp; drain and crumble.

To make dressing: Combine all ingredients in jar. Shake well. Chill. Remove garlic before serving.
In large salad bowl, toss spinach and bacon with desired amount of dressing. Garnish with egg. Serve immediately.

Chocolate Mousse

SERVES 8

1 6-ounce package chocolate chips
½ ounce bitter chocolate
6 eggs, separated
2 tablespoons brandy, Cointreau, Amaretto, etc.
⅓ teaspoon salt

Melt chocolates in top of double boiler over simmering water.
Beat egg yolks until thickened and lemon colored. Add chocolate and brandy; beat until smooth. Set aside.
Beat egg whites and salt until stiff, but not dry, peaks form. Fold into chocolate mixture. Spoon into eight ½-cup ramekins. Chill well.

TASTE OF INDIA DINNER

for Eight

＊Masala Shrimp (Spicy Shrimp)

＊Sial Gosht (Lamb in Yogurt)

＊Bhuna Chaval (Bommaloe) (Rice with Bombay Duck)

＊Spinach Raita (Spinach and Yogurt Sauce)

＊Tomato Chutney

＊Indian-Style Salad

＊Gajar Ka Halva (Carrot Dessert)

Beer

Ceremonial Bowl, late nineteenth century
Carved wood, Admiralty Islands
Gift of Dominique and John de Menil

Masala Shrimp
(Spicy Shrimp)

SERVES 8 as hors d'oeuvres
or 4 as entrée with rice

2   tablespoons vegetable oil
1   pound medium-size shrimp, shelled and
    deveined
¾   teaspoon salt
1   teaspoon ground coriander
½   teaspoon ground turmeric
½   teaspoon ground red chilies
¾   cup fresh lemon juice
½   cup chopped fresh cilantro

Heat oil in large skillet until very hot.
Add shrimp, salt, coriander, turmeric, and
chilies; sauté briskly about 5 minutes or
until shrimp turn opaque. Remove from
heat. Add lemon juice and cilantro. Toss to
mix well.

Serve at room temperature with tooth-
picks to skewer shrimp. Flavor will improve
if shrimp are cooked about ½ hour before
serving.

Sial Gosht
(Lamb in Yogurt)

SERVES 8

2   medium onions, finely chopped
2   tomatoes, skinned and finely chopped
1   1-inch piece fresh gingerroot, finely
    chopped
1   cup chopped fresh cilantro
3   teaspoons ground coriander
1   teaspoon ground red chilies
¾   teaspoon ground turmeric
1   teaspoon salt or more to taste
1   teaspoon ground cumin
¼   teaspoon each ground cinnamon, cloves,
    and cardamom
2   chilies serranos (fresh, hot), finely
    chopped (optional)
1   cup unflavored yogurt
2   tablespoons vegetable oil
½   cup water as needed
2   pounds boneless lamb, fat removed, cut
    into ½-inch cubes

Mix all ingredients except lamb and water to make marinade. Stir in lamb, tossing
well to cover. Add water and mix well.
Cover with plastic wrap. Marinate in glass
bowl at least 1 hour.

Transfer to large enamel or stainless steel
heavy pot. Cover; cook on low heat about
1½ hours or until meat is tender. Taste to
adjust seasonings.

May be cooked day or two before serving. Refrigerate. When ready to serve,
small amount of water may be added if too
thick. Serve over rice or with pita bread.

Variation: Venison may be substituted
for lamb.

Bhuna Chaval (Bommaloe)
(Rice with Bombay Duck)

SERVES 8

½   cup ghee (clarified butter)
1   small onion, finely chopped
2   cups basmati rice, washed and drained
     (Texmati or brown rice* may be
     substituted)
4   cups boiling water
1   teaspoon salt
1 to 2 teaspoons vegetable oil
1   ounce (scant) Bombay duck,** enough
     to make ½ cup, fried and crumbled

In heavy saucepan with tightly fitting lid,
heat ghee or clarified butter. Add onion
and fry 7 to 8 minutes or until golden
brown. Add rice and continue to fry additional 10 minutes, lifting and stirring constantly until golden. Add water and salt.
Increase heat and bring to boil. Reduce
heat to very low, cover tightly; cook 25
minutes or until rice is tender and liquid is
absorbed. Fluff with fork.

To serve with Bombay duck: Heat vegetable
oil until very hot but not smoking. Drop
in Bombay duck and fry until crisp. Drain
on paper towels. Crumble and scatter over
rice.

  * If using brown rice, increase water to 6
cups; cook, covered, 50 minutes.
  ** Available in specialty shops.

Spinach Raita
(Spinach and Yogurt Sauce)

SERVES 6 TO 8

1   pound fresh spinach
2   cups unflavored yogurt
Salt to taste
⅛   teaspoon ground cumin

  Blanch spinach in rapidly boiling water
2 to 3 minutes. Drain and press out all excess moisture. Cool and chop coarsely. Stir
in yogurt, adding salt to taste. Put mixture
in small bowl and sprinkle ground cumin
on top. Serve at room temperature.

Tomato Chutney

MAKES ABOUT 5 HALF-PINTS

1   1-inch piece fresh gingerroot
18   cloves garlic, peeled
1   teaspoon caraway seeds
1¾   cups cider vinegar, divided
2   1-pound, 10-ounce cans tomatoes, in-
     cluding liquid
6   green chilies serranos, seeded and
     chopped
1½   cups sugar
2   tablespoons golden raisins
1   tablespoon slivered blanched almonds
2   2-inch sticks cinnamon
8 to 10 whole peppercorns
½   teaspoon ground red chilies (Cayenne
     may be substituted)
8   whole cloves

  In blender or processor, grind gingerroot, garlic, and caraway seeds with a little
vinegar. Combine mixture with tomatoes
and remaining vinegar. Add remaining ingredients. Cook over low heat, stirring occasionally, until mixture thickens and turns
darker (1½ to 2 hours). Bottle in sterilized
jars.

Indian-Style Salad

SERVES 8

2   large red onions, very thinly sliced
2   large tomatoes, peeled, seeded if desired,
    and thinly sliced
3   cucumbers, peeled, scored lengthwise
    with fork, and thinly sliced
Juice of ½ large lemon
Salt to taste
Freshly cracked pepper to taste

Soak onions in ice water 1 hour. Remove
and pat dry. Layer onions, tomatoes, and
cucumbers in glass bowl.

Add lemon juice, salt, and pepper
about 30 minutes before serving. Do not
refrigerate.

Gajar Ka Halva
(Carrot Dessert)

SERVES 8

1½ pounds carrots, peeled and grated
1   quart whole milk
1¼ cups sugar
½   cup vegetable oil or butter
¼   cup raisins
6   cardamom pods, seeds only, crushed, or
     ¼ teaspoon ground cardamom
¼   cup slivered blanched almonds
Silver sheet to decorate (optional) *

Combine carrots and milk in heavy
saucepan. Cook on medium heat, stirring
occasionally, until mixture begins to
thicken (can take up to 1 hour). Reduce
heat during last 15 minutes.

Add sugar, oil, and raisins. Cook, stirring constantly, until mixture begins to
leave sides of pan. Do not allow it to stick
to bottom (may take 15 to 20 minutes).

Remove to platter, mounding mixture in
center. Garnish with cardamom seeds and
almonds. Spread silver sheet over top if
desired.

*Available in specialty shops.

Black Lion Wharf, *1859*
Etching and drypoint by James Abbott McNeill Whistler
Gift of Marjorie G. and Evan C. Horning

"AFTER THE OPENING"
BROILED SHRIMP DINNER

for Six

✶ Cheese Straws

✶ Mushrooms Stuffed with Spinach

✶ Broiled Shrimp with Garlic

✶ Green Rice

✶ Tomatoes with Curry

French Bread (see p. 143)

✶ Crêpes with Orange Sauce

Bring friends home for an elegant supper after the art exhibit preview party. The cheese straws are ready to serve with drinks. Mushrooms are assembled and waiting to be removed from the refrigerator and heated. Shrimp are skewered and ready to broil while the tomatoes bake and the rice is reheated in a double boiler. Crêpes are stuffed and arranged in an oven-to-table serving dish. It remains now to heat the sauce and finish the dessert. Bon appétit.

Cheese Straws

YIELDS 42 CHEESE STRAWS 4 INCHES
LONG

½   cup solid vegetable shortening
¼   cup boiling water
1¼ cups flour
½   teaspoon baking powder
1   teaspoon salt
½   teaspoon paprika
⅛   teaspoon ground Cayenne pepper or to
     taste
½   cup grated sharp Cheddar cheese
½   cup grated Parmesan cheese

Place shortening in bowl; add boiling water. With fork, first stir and then beat until all water is absorbed and mixture is light and creamy. Sift flour with baking powder, salt, paprika, and pepper. Combine with shortening. Stir with fork only until dough forms smooth ball. Blend in cheeses. Wrap in waxed paper; chill until firm.

Preheat oven to 450°.

Roll dough between two sheets lightly floured waxed paper into rectangle approximately 8 × 11 inches. Trim edges. Cut horizontally with sharp knife or pastry wheel into 2 rectangles (each 4 × 11 inches). Cut each into 21 half-inch strips. Place on baking sheet; bake about 15 minutes.

Mushrooms Stuffed with Spinach

SERVES 6

18 medium-size firm white mushrooms
2   tablespoons butter, divided
2   tablespoons finely chopped onion
1   small clove garlic, pressed
¼   cup Parmesan cheese
½   cup cottage cheese
½   cup spinach, washed, blanched, and
     squeezed dry
¼   teaspoon freshly grated nutmeg
1   teaspoon chopped fresh marjoram or
     ½ teaspoon dried marjoram
2   tablespoons sherry
Salt and pepper to taste
Coarse salt

Preheat oven to 350°.

Wipe mushrooms clean with damp cloth. Carefully remove stems and reserve.

Melt 1 tablespoon butter in pie pan or small skillet. Roll mushroom caps in butter to coat. Bake, stem side down, in oven 10 minutes. Set aside.

Chop reserved mushroom stems finely; sauté in small skillet with onion and garlic in remaining butter until translucent. Do not brown. Place onion mixture, cheeses, spinach, and seasonings in processor or blender; mix thoroughly. Taste and correct seasonings.

Discard liquid accumulated in pan with mushroom caps. Sprinkle caps with a little coarse salt; stuff them with spinach mixture, mounding the filling. Heat in oven 10 minutes. Serve immediately.

Variation: Minced ham or bacon bits can be added to mixture, or ¼ teaspoon jalapeño jelly can be spread over each cap before final heating.

Broiled Shrimp with Garlic

SERVES 6

To serve six, use 5 shrimp per serving (16 to 18 per pound size). Shell them raw; leave tails intact; arrange on 6 thin wooden or metal skewers.

Sauce:
8   tablespoons butter
⅓   cup olive oil
1   lemon, juice and grated zest
2 or 3 large cloves garlic, pressed
1   tablespoon chopped fresh tarragon or 1 teaspoon dried tarragon
Freshly ground black pepper
Coarse salt
2   tablespoons finely chopped parsley for garnish

Over low heat melt butter. Remove pan from heat; stir in olive oil, lemon juice and zest, garlic, tarragon, and pepper.

Put shrimp on skewers in oven-proof gratin dish in one layer. Pour sauce over shrimp. Turn skewers until thoroughly coated.

Preheat broiler to highest temperature. Sprinkle shrimp with a little coarse salt. Place on rack 3 or 4 inches below heat. Broil about 5 minutes, basting once. Turn skewers over; sprinkle again with salt. Broil additional 5 minutes. (Shrimp should be bright pink, slightly browned, with tails almost blackened.)

Sprinkle with chopped parsley. Serve immediately on bed of green rice. Spoon sauce over each serving.

Green Rice

SERVES 6

1   cup long-grain rice
4   tablespoons butter
6   scallions, including some green tops, finely chopped
¼   cup finely chopped parsley
Salt to taste

Drop rice into 2 quarts rapidly boiling salted water. Lower heat; simmer about 20 minutes, uncovered, until rice is tender. Drain into colander; immediately place uncovered colander over simmering water.

Meanwhile, melt butter in large skillet. Sauté scallions and parsley until soft. Add rice. Toss gently until well mixed. Taste for salt.

Tomatoes with Curry

SERVES 6

3   medium-size firm, ripe tomatoes
6   tablespoons sour cream
6   tablespoons homemade mayonnaise (see p. 223)
1   teaspoon curry powder
Salt
Chopped parsley for garnish

Preheat oven to 350°.

Cut tomatoes in half; gently remove seeds and watery part around them. Drain, inverted, a few minutes while mixing topping.

Combine cream, mayonnaise, and curry powder. Sprinkle tomatoes lightly with salt. Spoon filling into tomato halves. Bake about 20 minutes or until topping puffs and begins to brown. Serve with sprinkling of parsley.

Crêpes with Orange Sauce

YIELDS 30 CRÊPES

1   cup cold water
1   cup cold milk
4   eggs
½   teaspoon salt
2   cups sifted flour
4   tablespoons melted butter
Vegetable oil

Filling (serves 6):
1½ cups creamed cottage cheese
1   egg
2   tablespoons sugar
1   teaspoon grated orange zest
12 crêpes

Orange Sauce:
2   tablespoons cornstarch
1   cup sugar
¼   teaspoon salt
2   cups orange juice
Sour cream
2   cups orange sections

To make crêpes: Put water, milk, and eggs in blender or food processor. Add salt, flour, and butter. Process about 1 minute. Use rubber spatula to clean flour off sides of blender. Process again briefly. Refrigerate batter at least 2 hours before using.

Use 5- or 7-inch crêpe pan. Brush with vegetable oil; heat until almost smoking. Pour scant ¼ cup batter into pan. Immediately tilt pan in all directions to cover bottom. Pour any batter that does not adhere back into bowl. Return pan to fire for 1 minute. Turn crêpe over and fry other side. Use second side as inside of crêpe. Continue until all batter is used. Crêpes can be frozen with waxed paper between them.

To make filling: Combine cottage cheese, egg, sugar, and orange zest in small bowl. Beat by hand or in processor or blender until smooth. Spoon about 3 tablespoons filling into center of each crêpe. Roll; place in single layer in baking dish or in six individual oval gratins.

To make sauce: Preheat oven to 350°.

In medium saucepan, mix cornstarch, sugar, salt, and orange juice. Cook over medium heat, stirring constantly, until mixture thickens and comes to boil. Simmer 1 minute. Remove from heat; add orange sections. Spoon small amount of sauce over crêpes. Bake until sauce bubbles. Serve immediately with sour cream and hot orange sections.

AN EASTER LUNCH

for Eight

⁎ Cold Zucchini Soup

⁎ Butterflied Leg of Lamb

⁎ Tomato Cases with Broccoli Florets

⁎ Kasha with Onions and Mushrooms

⁎ Apricot Mousse

Rioja Reserva

Sheep, nineteenth century
Painted wood, Artist unknown
Bayou Bend Collection, Gift of Miss Ima Hogg

Cold Zucchini Soup

SERVES 8

5 to 6 medium zucchini
1   large onion, peeled and thinly sliced
     (about 1 cup)
½   teaspoon curry powder
2   ribs celery with leaves, finely chopped
¼   teaspoon salt
¼   teaspoon ground pepper
3   cups strong chicken broth, preferably
     homemade (see p. 221) *
1   cup milk or half-and-half
Finely chopped chives for garnish

Rinse zucchini and dry. Remove ends. Slice one zucchini into matchstick strips about 1½ inches long. Blanch strips in boiling water 2 minutes. Drain; refresh with cold water. Drain and set aside.

Cut remaining zucchini into ½-inch cubes. Place in saucepan with onion slices, curry powder, celery, salt, and pepper. Add chicken broth. Bring to boil. Reduce heat; simmer 45 minutes.

Allow mixture to cool slightly. Place in processor or blender in batches; purée until smooth. Chill.

Before serving, stir in milk or cream and zucchini strips. Taste for seasonings. Garnish with chopped chives.

*If using canned chicken broth, fortify with chicken bouillon cubes, granules, or powder to taste. Do not add salt.

Butterflied Leg of Lamb

SERVES 8

1   leg of lamb (6 pounds), boned and
     butterflied
1   clove garlic, pressed
¾   cup oil
¼   cup red wine vinegar
½   onion, chopped (about ½ cup)
2   teaspoons Dijon mustard
2   teaspoons salt
½   teaspoon dried oregano
½   teaspoon dried basil
⅛   teaspoon freshly ground pepper
1   bay leaf, crumbled

Place lamb fat side down in shallow pan. In small bowl mix all ingredients together; pour over lamb. Cover pan; refrigerate overnight, turning meat at least once. Remove from refrigerator 1 hour before cooking.

Preheat broiler and oven to 425°.

Put meat in broiler pan, skin side down. Broil about 4 inches from heat 10 minutes. Turn lamb; baste. Broil on other side 10 minutes. Transfer meat to oven; roast additional 10 minutes. Carve lamb into thin slices before serving.

Tomato Cases with Broccoli Florets

SERVES 8

8   ripe tomatoes (about 2½ inches
     diameter)
2   teaspoons salt
1   large bunch broccoli, allow about 6 flo-
     rets per tomato
7   tablespoons olive oil
2   cloves garlic
2   tablespoons lemon juice

Preheat oven to 350°.

Cut tops from tomatoes; remove pulp. Salt cavities. Invert tomatoes to drain.

Wash broccoli; cut florets with 1- to 1½-inch stems. Boil 3 minutes. Drain; refresh under running cold water.

Heat oil in sauce pan or wok. Add garlic; simmer 3 or 4 minutes. Remove garlic; sauté broccoli until hot. Add lemon juice; mix well. Remove broccoli from oil; set aside.

Brush interiors of tomatoes with some of seasoned oil. Arrange broccoli in tomato cases, with heads up, in glass or enamel baking dish. Bake in remaining oil 10 minutes.

Dish may be prepared ahead to the point of baking. Cover filled tomatoes with plastic wrap; refrigerate. Allow 2 to 3 minutes additional baking time for this method.

Kasha with Onions and Mushrooms

SERVES 8

6 tablespoons butter, divided
1½ cups kasha (coarse buckwheat)
½ onion, finely chopped (about ½ cup)
1 clove garlic, pressed
1 teaspoon seasoned salt
½ teaspoon freshly ground pepper
½ teaspoon ground mace
4 cups chicken stock (see p. 221)
½ cup tiny white onions, cooked and drained
1 cup sliced mushrooms
1 tablespoon chopped parsley for garnish

Melt 1 tablespoon butter in heavy skillet. Add kasha; cook over moderate heat 10 minutes, stirring constantly. Add 3 tablespoons butter, onion, garlic, seasonings, and stock. Cover; cook over low heat 25 minutes, stirring occasionally. If mixture becomes too dry, add more stock or water.

Meanwhile, in small skillet brown onions in 1 tablespoon butter. Remove onions. In same skillet, sauté mushrooms in remaining butter. Add onions and mushrooms to kasha mixture.

Preheat oven to 350°.

Pour mixture into baking-serving dish. Cover; bake 30 minutes or until tender but moist. Taste for seasoning. Fluff with fork. Garnish with parsley.

Apricot Mousse

SERVES 8 TO 10

1 cup sugar
1 cup water
6 ounces dried apricots
3 egg whites
⅛ teaspoon grated nutmeg
1 cup heavy cream, whipped
Whipped cream flavored with orange-flavored liqueur for garnish (optional)

Boil water and sugar until soft-ball stage is reached (240°).

Meanwhile, place apricots in heavy, small saucepan. Cover with water; simmer 10 minutes. Cool in pan. Do not drain.

Purée apricots in processor or blender until smooth. Measure. If not 2 cups, add water to make 2 cups.

Beat egg whites until firm peaks form. Add hot syrup slowly, continuing to beat until cool. Add apricot purée and nutmeg. Mix thoroughly.

Whip cream until stiff. Fold into mixture.

Oil decorative 8-cup mold. Pour mousse into mold. Cover; freeze at least 2 hours.

Unmold onto serving platter. Garnish with whipped cream flavored with orange-flavored liqueur if desired.

Eagle-Headed Winged Deity, 883–859 B.C.
Gypsum, Assyrian
Agnes Cullen Arnold Endowment Fund

SPRING SALAD BUFFET

for Twenty-five

⋆ Kir Royale

⋆ Curried Cashew Nuts

⋆ Seviche

⋆ Chicken Pasta Salad with Garlic-Avocado Dressing

⋆ Tropical Fruit Salad

⋆ Potato, Ham, and Cabbage Salad Platter

⋆ Duck Liver Pâté au Porto

Assorted Greens Vinaigrette (see p. 225)

⋆ Marinated Vegetable Salad Genovese

⋆ Tuscan Bread

⋆ Mousse au Chocolat Blanc with Chocolate Sauce

Five assorted salads—seafood, chicken, meat, mixed vegetables, and fruit—are offered, as well as crisp cold greens vinaigrette, accompanied by rich, smooth pâté. Bread and herb butter (see p. 222) will round out a complete party meal built around this unusual theme. Double the dessert recipe to make two separate molds of mousse. It is sinfully rich and keeps well if there are any leftovers. If the guest list expands to another half-dozen guests, this is a menu that will accommodate those extra few. Although each recipe serves 12 generously, the combination of all the salads will be sufficient for a larger group.

Kir Royale

In bottom of each flute champagne glass, pour ½ teaspoonful crème de cassis (black-currant liqueur). Fill glass with good, but not expensive, dry champagne.

Variation: Pour ½ teaspoonful Chambord (black-raspberry liqueur) over one fresh raspberry and fill with dry champagne.

Curried Cashew Nuts

YIELDS 3 CUPS

1 pound raw cashew nuts (about 3 cups)
1 tablespoon vegetable oil
1 teaspoon coarse kosher salt
1 tablespoon curry powder or to taste

Preheat oven to 250°.
Spread cashew nuts in large flat pan; bake about 1 hour or until dry and crisp.
Stir in oil, salt, and curry powder; mix well. Return to oven additional 45 minutes, stirring occasionally. Cool on paper towels.

Seviche

1½ to 2 pounds firm fish or shellfish (such as pompano, grouper, red fish, conch, or scallops), filleted, skinned, and cubed

Marinade:
Juice of 30 small Mexican limes (about 1½ cups)
½   teaspoon salt
1   teaspoon sugar
1   tablespoon vinegar
¼   teaspoon ground white pepper
2   tablespoons olive oil

Sauce:
1   tablespoon finely chopped parsley
1   medium-large onion, finely chopped
1   large clove garlic, pressed
8   large black olives, pitted and sliced
2   teaspoons light soy sauce
½   cup chili sauce
2   tablespoons finely chopped fresh oregano or 1 teaspoon dried oregano
½   bay leaf, finely crumbled
5   medium-ripe tomatoes, peeled, seeded, and finely chopped (if not red and juicy enough, add ¼ cup clam-tomato juice)
2   tablespoons lime juice
1   teaspoon salt
1 to 2 teaspoons sugar
1   teaspoon Tabasco sauce

Put cubed seafood in bowl and cover with marinade, adding more lime juice if necessary. Cover and refrigerate at least 1½ to 3 hours.

Make sauce by combining all ingredients; refrigerate.

Put fish in strainer and rinse well; then drain well. Mix cubed fish and sauce; refrigerate and serve ice cold. Finely cut hot Mexican pepper can be added to taste.

The longer the seafood remains in marinade the softer it will become, and the more pronounced flavor of lime will be.

Chicken Pasta Salad with Garlic-Avocado Dressing

8   chicken breasts, cooked, boned, skinned, and cubed
24   ounces shell pasta, cooked and rinsed with cool water
4   tablespoons olive oil
6   tablespoons finely chopped fresh parsley
8   tablespoons chopped green scallion tops
½ to 1 teaspoon salt
Freshly ground black pepper to taste

Dressing:
2   large eggs
2   tablespoons fresh lemon juice
5   tablespoons white wine vinegar
½   teaspoon dry mustard
½   teaspoon salt
1   teaspoon sugar
¼   teaspoon cayenne pepper
2   cloves garlic, peeled
1   cup vegetable oil
½   cup olive oil
2   large ripe avocados
Cherry tomatoes and thinly sliced red onion rings for garnish

Combine chicken, pasta, olive oil, parsley, scallions, salt, and pepper. Set aside.

To make dressing: Combine eggs, lemon juice, vinegar, dry mustard, salt, sugar, cayenne pepper, and garlic; process in blender or processor until smooth.

Combine vegetable oil and olive oil; add to mixture in slow steady stream to form emulsion.

Peel and chop avocados; blend into dressing until smooth. Taste to adjust seasonings.

If chicken-pasta mixture is refrigerated, allow time to reach room temperature before serving. Toss with dressing; garnish with cherry tomatoes and onion rings.

Tropical Fruit Salad

SERVES 12

6   bananas, sliced
4   avocados, sliced
8   kiwi fruits, sliced
2   mangos, sliced
2   papayas, sliced
½   cup toasted flaked coconut

Dressing (yields 1 cup):
⅓   cup orange juice
⅓   cup vegetable oil
3   tablespoons brown sugar
2   tablespoons light rum
½   teaspoon salt
½   teaspoon paprika
⅓   cup chopped or slivered toasted almonds
Red-tipped lettuce for garnish (optional)

Arrange fruits in attractive pattern on clear glass or plain white platter. May be garnished with red-tipped lettuce for color.

Shake combined dressing ingredients in tightly covered jar. Refrigerate at least 1 hour.

Spoon dressing over fruits; sprinkle with coconut. Dressing is enough to just cover fruit. If extra dressing is desired to serve separately, double recipe.

Potato, Ham, and Cabbage Salad Platter

SERVES 12

¼   cup dry vermouth
¼   cup white wine vinegar
1   clove garlic, crushed
1   teaspoon salt
1½   cups olive oil
4   pounds waxy boiling potatoes
1   teaspoon salt
1   teaspoon freshly ground pepper
1   cup celery, thinly sliced
1   cup scallions including green tops, thinly sliced
⅔   cup finely chopped parsley
2   cups cooked ham cut into thin strips (about 1 pound)
4   cups red cabbage, finely shredded (about 1 pound), reserve 4 outside leaves to garnish
1   cup green bell pepper, thinly sliced
¼   cup finely chopped chives
Additional salt and pepper to taste

Combine vermouth, vinegar, garlic, and salt; shake to mix well. Add olive oil, mix well, set aside.

Boil potatoes until tender but still firm. Skin and slice into ½-inch slices. Pour salt, pepper, and ⅔ of dressing over slices; toss gently. Cool to room temperature. Add celery, scallions, parsley, and ham. Mix well. Taste to correct seasonings.

Combine cabbage, green bell pepper, and chives. Add remaining dressing; salt and pepper to taste.

To serve, mound potato salad in center of large platter inside reserved red cabbage leaves. Surround with ring of cabbage–green bell pepper salad.

Note: Cabbage–green bell pepper salad should be made on day to be served to retain bright colors.

Duck Liver Pâté au Porto

YIELDS AROUND 6 CUPS

1   pound duck livers (chicken livers may be substituted)
1   teaspoon salt
1   teaspoon freshly ground white pepper
1   cup port wine
4   ounces cooked ham, ground
2   ounces slab bacon, rind removed, ground
8   ounces pork (not too lean), ground
2   tablespoons crème fraîche (see p. 222)
1   large egg, beaten
2   shallots, finely chopped
1½ teaspoons grated orange zest
Bacon for lining terrine, blanched
1   bay leaf

Clean livers and place in nonmetallic bowl. Salt and pepper them, cover with wine and refrigerate overnight.

Preheat oven to 375°.

Remove livers from marinade, saving liquid. Purée livers in processor, in blender, or through fine sieve. Add ham, bacon, and pork, mixing well. Add crème fraîche, egg, shallots, and zest, using some of marinade to work mixture to loose doughlike consistency. Cook spoonful of mixture in a little butter to check for seasonings. Should be fairly highly seasoned.

Line 7-cup (9 × 5 × 3–inch) terrine with blanched bacon strips, leaving ends hanging over sides of terrine. Spoon in liver mixture. Place bay leaf on top and fold over ends of bacon to cover top. Cover tightly with foil and bake 1 to 1½ hours or until juices run clear.

Remove from oven and weight top (a brick covered in foil is good). Leave on counter to cool 2 to 3 hours. Store in refrigerator, weighted, overnight.

Serve with Melba toast or unsalted crackers.

Marinated Vegetable Salad Genovese

SERVES 8 TO 10

4   cups thinly sliced zucchini
2   cups thinly sliced yellow squash
2   cups broccoli florets
1½ cups bite-size cauliflower florets
1   cup thinly sliced carrots
1   cup thinly sliced purple onion
1   cup halved cherry tomatoes

Dressing:
1   cup vegetable oil
½   cup white wine vinegar
¼   cup red wine vinegar
¼   cup lemon juice
1   teaspoon salt
1   teaspoon finely chopped fresh oregano or ½ teaspoon dried oregano
1   teaspoon dry mustard
1   teaspoon finely chopped onion
1   small clove garlic, pressed
½   teaspoon crushed anise seed

To make dressing: Combine all ingredients in jar; shake well until salt dissolves.

Combine sliced raw vegetables with dressing. Refrigerate salad several hours, stirring occasionally. May be kept several days in refrigerator.

Tuscan Bread

YIELDS 1 LARGE LOAF

Sponge:
2   packages active dry yeast
¼   cup warm water (110°)
9   tablespoons unbleached flour (½ cup
     plus 1 tablespoon), divided

Dough:
6   or more cups unbleached flour
1   teaspoon salt
1½ cups warm water, divided

To make sponge: Dissolve yeast in warm water.

Place 8 tablespoons (½ cup) flour in bowl; beat in yeast with wooden spoon. Mix until small ball of dough forms. Sprinkle with remaining flour. Cover with cloth. Place in warm, draft-free spot; allow to double in size (about 1 hour).

To make dough: Mound 6 cups flour on work surface. Make a well in center; add sponge, salt, and ½ cup water. Mix ingredients in the well carefully, using wooden spoon. Add remaining water. Gradually mix in enough flour to form medium-firm dough.

Knead dough until smooth and elastic, adding more flour as necessary to keep it from being sticky. (Proportion of flour to water will vary according to humidity.) Dough may be made in heavy-duty mixer by combining sponge with all of water and salt and gradually adding flour.

Form dough into large round loaf. Wrap loosely in well-floured dish towel. Place in warm, draft-free spot. Allow to rise second time until doubled in size (about 1 hour).

To bake: For best crust, cover middle shelf of oven with unglazed terra-cotta tiles and preheat 400° 20 minutes. When loaf has doubled in size, turn directly onto tiles. Bread will fall a bit but will rise a third time in oven, giving a very light texture. Bake 50 to 60 minutes or until bottom of loaf sounds hollow when tapped. Do not open oven door first 30 minutes of baking or bread will fall.

If tiles are not available, sprinkle cornmeal on heavy cookie sheet or pizza tile. Place loaf directly onto surface. Do not wrap; cover loosely with cloth. Place in warm, draft-free spot. Allow to rise until doubled in size. Slash in several places with razor about ½ inch deep. Bake 50 to 60 minutes or until loaf sounds hollow when tapped.

When baked, cool bread on wire rack 2 to 3 hours before cutting.

Mousse au Chocolat Blanc
with Chocolate Sauce

SERVES 12 TO 18

Crust:

8	ounces chocolate wafer cookies
6	tablespoons butter

Mousse:

12	ounces white chocolate
½	cup boiling water
2	tablespoons white crème de cacao
4	large eggs, separated
3	cups whipping cream
⅛	teaspoon salt
⅛	teaspoon cream of tartar
¾	cup sugar
1 to 2	ounces semisweet chocolate for decoration

Chocolate Sauce (yields 2 cups):

6	ounces unsweetened chocolate
¾	cup sugar
¼	teaspoon salt
1½	tablespoons butter
1½	cups cream
1	tablespoon vanilla extract (see p. 224) or 1 to 2 tablespoons liqueur or rum

Preheat oven to 375°.

To make crust: Crush cookies until fine crumbs.

Melt butter; add cookie crumbs, mixing well.

Using 10-inch spring-form pan, butter sides only. Press layer of crumb mixture evenly over bottom. Tilt pan at 45° angle, turning to coat sides with mixture. Bake 7 to 8 minutes. Set aside to cool completely.

To make mousse: Break or grate chocolate into small pieces. Cover with boiling water. Stir until smooth. Cool slightly; add crème de cacao. Beat in egg yolks, one at a time, until completely smooth.

Whip cream until soft but not stiff peaks form. Set aside.

Beat egg whites until frothy. Add salt and cream of tartar; beat until soft peaks form. Reduce speed; gradually add sugar. Increase speed; beat a few minutes until meringue is quite firm.

Fold chocolate mixture into meringue; then fold in whipped cream. Spoon into cooled crust.

Place in freezer. When firm, cover with plastic wrap. Freeze overnight or up to 3 weeks.

Cut around sides of crust with thin knife, pressing firmly against pan. Release pan sides; cut under crust with spatula. Slide mousse onto service plate.

Melt semisweet chocolate over low heat. Dribble decorative pattern over top of mousse. Return to freezer to firm chocolate decoration.

To make chocolate sauce: Chop chocolate coarsely; place over lowest possible heat in heavy saucepan. Stir frequently until chocolate melts. Stir in sugar, salt, and butter. Add cream, stirring until smooth. Increase heat; cook constantly for about 5 minutes or until sauce thickens slightly, stirring constantly.

Remove from heat; stir in vanilla extract or other flavoring. Sauce will keep several weeks in refrigerator. Before serving, reheat in double boiler over hot water.

The Carp
Woodblock print by Keisai Eisen
Lent by Marjorie G. and Evan C. Horning

PATIO DINNER

for Six

＊Clear Mushroom Soup

＊Charcoaled Baked Redfish

＊Eggplant Rollatini

Green Salad

＊Pecan Crunch

Fumé Blanc

Clear Mushroom Soup

SERVES 6

2   tablespoons butter
2 to 3 shallots, finely chopped
1½   pounds fresh mushrooms, very finely
      chopped
6   cups rich chicken broth (see p. 221)
½   teaspoon salt
1   teaspoon lemon juice
1   lemon, thinly sliced

Heat butter in large saucepan. Add shallots; cook over medium heat until transparent (about 3 minutes). Add mushrooms and cook additional 5 minutes, stirring occasionally. Add chicken broth; bring to boil. Reduce heat; simmer uncovered 30 minutes.

Skim off excess fat. Strain soup through coarse sieve, pressing mushrooms firmly to extract all liquid. Allow some specks of mushroom to go through.

Season with salt and lemon juice. Garnish with lemon slices.

Charcoaled Baked Redfish

SERVES 6

Build hot fire in covered barbecue grill, placing rack 4 to 6 inches above coals.

3   pounds redfish, filleted
10   tablespoons lemon or lime juice
6   tablespoons butter, softened
2   small cloves garlic, pressed
5   scallions, finely chopped
¾   teaspoon salt
½   teaspoon cracked pepper

Place fish in pan in single layer or make pan out of aluminum foil, rolling up edges to hold juices. Pour lemon or lime juice over fish. Let stand 30 minutes, turning frequently.

Meanwhile, mix butter and garlic until blended. Sprinkle scallions on fish. Add salt and pepper. Spread garlic butter over fillets.

Place fish on rack in grill; cover and bake 20 minutes.

Test fish to see if it flakes. If not, cook a few minutes more. Serve immediately, pouring pan juices over fish. It will not be browned, but juices will be golden.

Eggplant Rollatini

SERVES 6

2   eggplants (about 1 pound each)
½   teaspoon salt
1½ to 2 tablespoons olive oil
1½   cups cottage cheese
1   cup freshly grated Parmesan cheese, divided
3   tablespoons fresh basil or 1½ teaspoons dried basil
1   clove garlic
⅛   teaspoon grated nutmeg
Chopped parsley for garnish

Tomato Sauce:
1   large onion, finely chopped (about 1 cup)
½   large green bell pepper, finely chopped (about ½ cup)
2   tablespoons butter
4 to 5 fresh tomatoes, peeled, seeded, and chopped (about 2 cups)
½   teaspoon salt
Bouquet garni: 2 to 3 sprigs each of thyme, marjoram, and parsley or ½ teaspoon each, dried, tied up in cheesecloth or garni bag

Preheat oven to 350°.

Slice eggplant lengthwise into ¼ to ½-inch slices. Salt lightly on both sides and leave in colander to drain ½ hour. Rinse and dry thoroughly with paper towels. Arrange in one layer on baking sheet.

Brush well with olive oil. Broil in oven until golden. Turn, brush other side with oil and broil until browned and soft. Cool.

Drain cottage cheese well in colander, pressing lightly to remove as much liquid as possible. In processor or blender combine cottage cheese, ½ cup Parmesan cheese, basil, garlic, and nutmeg. Blend until smooth.

Spread cheese mixture evenly on eggplant slices. Roll lengthwise, starting at narrow end. Arrange rolls in one layer in 8 × 11–inch gratin pan.

To make sauce: In heavy saucepan sauté onion and green pepper in butter until soft. Add tomatoes, salt, and bouquet garni. Cook, covered, about 10 minutes over low heat. Uncover; stir.

Raise heat to medium, cooking additional 10 minutes or until most of liquid has evaporated. Correct seasoning and discard bouquet garni.

Pour 1½ cups tomato sauce over rolls. Sprinkle with remaining Parmesan cheese. Bake 20 to 25 minutes or until sauce is bubbling and cheese is golden brown. Garnish with chopped parsley.

Pecan Crunch

SERVES 6 TO 8

3   eggs
½   teaspoon baking powder
1   cup sugar
11   double graham crackers, crushed
1   cup chopped pecans
1   teaspoon vanilla extract (see p. 224)

Topping:
1   cup whipping cream
2   tablespoons Amaretto
1   teaspoon sugar

Preheat oven to 350°.

Beat eggs and baking powder. Gradually add sugar. Beat until very stiff. Fold graham crackers, pecans, and vanilla extract into egg mixture.

Spread in heavily buttered 10-inch pie pan. Bake 30 minutes. Remove from oven. Chill in refrigerator at least 4 to 5 hours.

To make topping: Whip cream. Blend Amaretto and sugar into whipped cream. Spread on chilled pie.

Window, San Antonio, Texas, *1918*
Platinum print by Paul Strand
Museum purchase

WARM SPRING NIGHT SUPPER

for Four

＊Cold Marinated Beef Tenderloin

＊Cold Pasta Salad with Pesto

French Bread (see p. 143) with Herb Butter (see p. 222)

＊Chocolate-Orange Bars

Beaujolais

Cold Marinated Beef Tenderloin

SERVES 4 TO 6

1½ pounds tenderloin of beef
1 teaspoon vegetable oil
⅓ cup fruit-flavored vinegar
1 teaspoon salt
1 teaspoon water-packed canned or freeze-dried green peppercorns, crushed
2 tablespoons finely chopped chives
1 teaspoon fresh tarragon or ½ teaspoon dried tarragon
1 teaspoon fresh thyme or ½ teaspoon dried thyme
1 clove garlic, pressed
1 teaspoon Dijon mustard
⅔ cup olive oil
1 whole pimiento, thinly sliced
1 rib celery, thinly sliced
1 small purple onion, thinly sliced
¼ pound fresh snow peas, strings and tops removed
Red-tipped lettuce for garnish
12 cherry tomatoes for garnish

Preheat oven to 450°.

Roll meat; tie securely. Pat dry.

Heat oil in heavy skillet until smoking. Brown meat on all sides. Roast 15 minutes or until internal temperature reaches 120°. Remove from pan; place on rack to cool to room temperature.

Meanwhile, combine vinegar, salt, peppercorns, herbs, garlic, and mustard. Blend until salt dissolves. Stir in oil; pour over sliced vegetables.

Remove strings from cooled meat; slice as thinly as possible, no thicker than ¼ inch. Layer meat and vegetables in container; cover with dressing. Allow to marinate several hours.

Arrange leaves of red-tipped lettuce in bowl. Mound meat and vegetables in center. Garnish with cherry tomatoes.

Cold Pasta Salad with Pesto

SERVES 4

4 cups cooked pasta (linguine, conchiglie, vermicelli, etc.; about 8 ounces dried)
¾ cup pesto (see p. 223)
1 tablespoon butter
1 tablespoon finely chopped shallots
¾ pound mushrooms, thinly sliced
1 10-ounce package frozen peas
½ cup sliced ripe olives
Salt and pepper to taste
1 tablespoon Parmesan cheese or to taste
Lettuce for garnish

Cook pasta in 4 quarts water with 1 tablespoon salt. Drain; add 2 cups cold water. Drain again; add pesto. Mix well; set aside.

Melt butter; add shallots. Sauté 1 minute. Add mushrooms; sauté 2 minutes. Drain; set aside.

Cook peas according to directions on package. Drain; set aside. When ready to serve, add peas, olives, mushroom-shallot mixture, salt, and pepper. Toss lightly; sprinkle with Parmesan cheese. Serve on lettuce-lined platter.

Chocolate-Orange Bars

YIELDS 8 DOZEN 1-INCH SQUARES

1¾ cups sifted flour, divided
1½ cups firmly packed light brown sugar,
    divided
1   tablespoon grated orange zest
½   teaspoon salt, divided
8   tablespoons butter
1   6-ounce package semisweet chocolate
    pieces
2   eggs
½   teaspoon baking powder
1   teaspoon vanilla extract (see p. 224)
1½ cups chopped walnuts

Preheat oven to 350°.

Combine 1½ cups flour, ½ cup brown sugar, orange zest, and ¼ teaspoon salt in large bowl. Cut in butter until mixture is crumbly.

Press evenly in bottom of 13 × 9 × 2–inch ungreased baking pan. Bake 10 minutes or until firm. Remove from oven.

Sprinkle chocolate pieces over layer in pan. Let stand about 2 minutes or until chocolate softens. Spread evenly over pastry to make second layer.

In medium-sized bowl beat eggs until thick. Stir in remaining brown sugar, flour, and salt. Add baking powder, vanilla extract, and walnuts. Stir. Spread over chocolate layer in pan.

Bake additional 20 minutes or until top is firm and golden. Cool completely in pan on wire rack. Cut into 1-inch squares.

Victorian Bouquet, *1850 – 1855*
Oil painting by Severin Roesen
Agnes Cullen Arnold Endowment Fund

48

for Twelve

Champagne

⋆ Smoked Salmon Butter

⋆ Curried Cream of Celery Soup

⋆ Carousel Mandarin Chicken Salad

⋆ Honey-Wheat Egg Braid

⋆ Oranges à la Grecque

Smoked Salmon Butter

YIELDS 1 TO 1½ CUPS

1   cup smoked salmon or lox trimmings
¼   pound butter, softened
1   3-ounce package cream cheese

Purée salmon or lox in processor or blender. Add butter and cream cheese; process until smooth. Remove mixture from container; push through fine sieve to remove all tendons and skin.

Pack in 2-cup mold; refrigerate several hours until firm. Serve with thinly sliced pumpernickel, wheat, or rye bread or crackers.

Carousel Mandarin Chicken Salad

SERVES 12

6   cups diced cooked chicken
2   cups finely chopped celery
4   tablespoons fresh lemon juice
2   tablespoons finely chopped onion
2   teaspoons salt
⅔   cup mayonnaise (see p. 223)
2   cups seedless grapes
2   11-ounce cans mandarin oranges, drained
1   cup slivered toasted almonds
Leaf lettuce for garnish
Additional mandarin orange slices for garnish (optional)

Combine chicken, celery, lemon juice, onion, and salt. Chill several hours or overnight. Add mayonnaise, grapes, oranges, and almonds to chicken mixture. Toss well. Serve on lettuce. Garnish with additional orange slices if desired.

Curried Cream of Celery Soup

SERVES 12

6   tablespoons butter
16   celery ribs, thinly sliced (about 8 to 10 cups)
4   medium onions, chopped (about 2 cups)
2   tablespoons curry powder
2   quarts strong beef stock (see p. 220) or 2 10¾-ounce cans consommé plus 1 can water
4   egg yolks
4   cups cream
½   teaspoon salt or to taste
Cubed apples for garnish

Melt butter in large, heavy saucepan. Add celery and onions; sauté over moderate heat until golden (about 20 minutes). Stir in curry powder; cook over low heat 2 to 3 minutes. Pour in beef stock. Cover and simmer 30 to 40 minutes or until vegetables are very tender. Strain. Reserve broth.

In processor or blender purée vegetables with ½ cup broth until smooth. Return broth and vegetables to pan.

Blend egg yolks in cream in large bowl. Stir in 2 cups of hot soup. Combine egg liaison with remaining soup. Place over moderate heat, stirring constantly until thickened slightly. Serve hot or chilled garnished with apple cubes.

Honey-Wheat Egg Braid

YIELDS 1 LARGE LOAF

3 tablespoons active dry yeast
1 cup warm water
⅔ cup honey
2 teaspoons salt
1 cup melted butter
3 cups whole wheat flour
4 eggs, at room temperature
3 egg yolks, at room temperature, divided
1 teaspoon vanilla extract (see p. 224)
4 cups (approximately) unsifted white flour
½ cup wheat germ
2 tablespoons milk
Poppy or sesame seeds

Sprinkle yeast into warm water (105° to 110° F) in large, warm bowl. Stir until dissolved. Add honey, salt, butter, and whole wheat flour. Beat until smooth. Add eggs, 2 egg yolks, and vanilla extract. Beat until smooth. While stirring mixture, add enough white flour to make soft dough, adding wheat germ gradually.

On lightly floured board, knead dough until smooth and elastic, at least 10 minutes by hand. (Bread doughs that contain honey are sticky compared to doughs that contain sugar.)

Place dough in greased bowl, turning to grease top. Cover; let rise in warm draft-free location until doubled in bulk. Punch down dough. Cover bowl with plastic wrap. Refrigerate at least 5 hours or overnight.

On lightly floured surface, cut dough into three equal pieces. Roll each piece into long, tapered cylinder. Lay three ropes of dough on greased and floured sheet. Start to braid loosely from center to end. Then braid other side from center to end. (Divide dough into 6 cylinders to make 2 smaller loaves.) Cover and let rise in draft-free place until about double in bulk.

Blend remaining egg yolk and milk; brush mixture on loaf. Sprinkle with poppy seeds or sesame seeds.

Preheat oven to 350°.

Bake bread 30 to 35 minutes or until done. Remove from baking sheet. Cool on wire racks.

Oranges à la Grecque

SERVES 12

12 large oranges
Water to cover zest of oranges
3 cups sugar
12 cloves
¾ cup Grand Marnier or other orange-flavored liqueur

Thinly pare zest from 6 oranges. (Do not include white part, or pith, of orange.) With sharp knife cut zest into very thin strips. Place strips in small saucepan; cover with water. Cook zest until tender. Remove from pan.

Peel all oranges; remove white pith. Place oranges in bowl and set aside.

Combine 2 cups water, sugar, and cloves in saucepan. Bring to boil; continue boiling until caramel in color. Remove from heat. Cool slightly; stir in Grand Marnier.

Top each orange with sliced zest. Pour syrup over top. Chill.

Remove from refrigerator 30 minutes to 1 hour before serving. Serve 1 orange per person on dessert plate with small knife and fork for easy sectioning.

The Fall of Man, *1549*
Oil on panel, Lucas Cranach the Younger
Edith A. and Percy S. Straus Collection

SUPPER BY THE POOL

for Four

*Cheese and Mushroom Canapés
*Curried Chicken Kabobs
*Mixed Fruit Chutney
*Zucchini Salad
*Fig Preserve Cake

Cheese and Mushroom Canapés

YIELDS 4 DOZEN

½ pound mushrooms, finely chopped
1 tablespoon butter
8 ounces cream cheese
1 teaspoon Worcestershire sauce
2 tablespoons finely chopped onion
1 clove fresh garlic, pressed
½ teaspoon salt or to taste
⅛ teaspoon ground white pepper
1 loaf thin-sliced, homemade-type bread
8 tablespoons butter, softened

Sauté mushrooms in butter. Mix with cream cheese, Worcestershire sauce, onion, garlic, salt, and pepper. Cut small rounds of bread. Toast one side. Spread untoasted side with butter. Top with mushroom mixture. Refrigerate or freeze. When ready to serve, broil until puffy and brown.

Curried Chicken Kabobs

SERVES 4

½ cup ground cocktail peanuts
1 tablespoon firmly packed light brown sugar
1 tablespoon curry powder
½ teaspoon crushed red pepper
2 tablespoons lemon juice
¼ cup soy sauce
1 clove garlic, pressed
3 whole chicken breasts, boned, skinned, and cut into 1-inch cubes

In glass bowl, combine ground peanuts, brown sugar, curry, pepper, lemon juice, soy sauce, and garlic. Add chicken cubes; toss to coat thoroughly. Cover and chill at least 3 hours.

Thread chicken on skewers. Grill over hot coals 8 to 12 minutes, turning frequently.

Mixed Fruit Chutney

YIELDS 6 PINTS

2 8-ounce packages mixed dried fruit (whole or bits)
2 8-ounce packages dried fruit—choice of apples, pears, peaches, or apricots
2 tart apples, peeled, seeded, and chopped (about 1½ cups)
1 purple onion, chopped (about ¾ cup)
1 piece gingerroot, 1 × 1½ inches, peeled and finely chopped
4 to 5 hot red chilies, seeded and finely chopped, or 1½ teaspoons crushed red pepper flakes
2 cloves garlic, pressed
1 cup raisins—if dried fruit includes raisins, substitute 1 cup fresh or dried fruit of choice
1 lemon, seeded and chopped, including rind
2½ cups white vinegar
2⅓ cups brown sugar
1 tablespoon mustard seed
1 tablespoon curry powder
1 tablespoon salt

Soak dried fruit in water 1 hour. Drain, reserving 1 cup liquid. If fruit is not precut, chop about two-thirds; slice remaining one-third into thin strips.

Combine apples, onion, gingerroot, chilies, garlic, raisins, and lemon.

Bring vinegar and sugar to boil in large pot. Add spices, fruit, and apple mixture. Cook slowly about 45 minutes, stirring often. Add reserved liquid, if needed.

Fruit should be tender but firm. Put in hot, sterilized jars.

Zucchini Salad

SERVES 4

Dressing:
½ cup white wine vinegar
⅓ cup olive oil
1 tablespoon sugar
1 tablespoon chopped fresh basil or ½ teaspoon dried basil
1 garlic clove, pressed
½ teaspoon salt
½ teaspoon pepper

Salad:
2 cups sliced zucchini
1 head romaine lettuce
2 tablespoons finely chopped scallions
1 large tomato, cut into thin wedges

Mix dressing ingredients together; refrigerate.

Blanch zucchini about 3 minutes; drain; refresh in cold water. Marinate zucchini in dressing. Cover; chill several hours or overnight.

When ready to serve, drain zucchini, reserving dressing. Place on lettuce; top with scallions. Arrange tomato wedges around zucchini; drizzle all with dressing.

Fig Preserve Cake

SERVES 16

12 tablespoons butter or margarine
2 cups sugar
4 eggs
3 cups flour
1 cup buttermilk
1 teaspoon baking soda
⅛ teaspoon salt
1 teaspoon ground allspice
1 teaspoon ground cloves
1 teaspoon grated nutmeg
1 teaspoon ground cinnamon
2 teaspoons vanilla extract (see p. 224)
2 cups fig preserves
2 cups chopped pecans

Preheat oven to 350°.

Cream butter and sugar. Add eggs one at a time, beating well after each addition. Add flour, 1 cup at a time, alternating with buttermilk, ⅓ cup at a time. Beat well. Add baking soda, salt, spices, and vanilla extract. Mix in fig preserves and pecans. (Blend preserves into a smooth consistency if of homemade variety with whole figs and juice.)

Bake in greased 10-inch tube pan 1½ hours. Cool in pan.

Cake is heavy and should be removed carefully from pan. Serve in thin slices because it is rich.

HIGH SCHOOL GRADUATION PARTY

for Twelve

* Bean Dip

* Guacamole Pie

* Marinated Chicken Salad

* Mexican Chocolate Cake

* Lemonade

Spirits run high when young people shed the cares of final exams and graduation. A Mexican lunch—or brunch—around the pool is as carefree as the occasion demands. All except one dish in this menu may be prepared the day before, leaving only the guacamole pie to be assembled the morning of the party. Have big baskets of toasted tortillas to scoop up bean dip and guacamole, put out pita bread to be filled with chicken salad by the guests themselves, and follow up with generous slices of cake. Ole!

Bean Dip

SERVES 10 TO 12

1   pound dried pinto beans
3   medium-size onions, chopped (about 2 cups)
4   cloves garlic, chopped
2   teaspoons ground cumin seed
½   cup bacon drippings
3½ teaspoons salt
Water
6   teaspoons chili powder
½   teaspoon Tabasco sauce
8   tablespoons margarine (optional)
6   ounces sharp Cheddar cheese, grated (optional)

Wash and sort beans. Cover with cold water; soak overnight.

Drain beans; put in large saucepan. Add onion, garlic, cumin, bacon drippings, and salt. Cover with hot water. Cover pan; simmer 3 hours, stirring occasionally. Add water as necessary.

Add chili powder; cook additional 2 hours or until beans are tender. Mash until almost smooth. Stir in Tabasco sauce. Serve warm with tortilla chips.

For a richer dish, add optional margarine and cheese.

Female figure, seventh–eighth century A.D.
Pre-Columbian, Huastec pottery
Gift of Mrs. Harry C. Hanszen

Guacamole Pie

SERVES 12

8   small or 4 large avocados, peeled, seeded, and cubed
6   tablespoons lime juice
¼   teaspoon salt
16 ounces sour cream
6   ounces picante sauce or to taste
6   ounces Monterey Jack cheese, grated
¼   cup finely chopped parsley
⅛   teaspoon paprika

Place avocados in 7 × 11–inch shallow serving dish; sprinkle with lime juice and salt. Spread sour cream evenly over avocados. Spoon picante sauce over cream. Add grated cheese, parsley, and paprika. Serve as side dish or as dip with toasted tortilla chips.

Marinated Chicken Salad

SERVES 12

6   cups cubed cooked breast of chicken
4   small jalapeño peppers, finely chopped (about 4 tablespoons)
2   cups sour cream
4   tablespoons mayonnaise (see p. 223)
2   ribs celery, finely chopped (about ⅔ cup)
4   scallions, including green tops, finely chopped
4   tablespoons lime juice
½   teaspoon salt or to taste
3   teaspoons ground cumin seed
12 pita breads

Mix all ingredients together thoroughly. Cover; chill 6 hours or overnight. Salad will fill 12 6-inch pita breads.

Variation: Fill tomato cups or avocado halves.

Mexican Chocolate Cake

SERVES 12 TO 24

8 tablespoons butter
½ cup vegetable oil
2 ounces unsweetened chocolate or 4 tablespoons cocoa
1 cup water
2 cups flour
1 teaspoon baking soda
2 cups sugar
½ cup sour milk (place 1½ teaspoons vinegar in ½ cup measure and fill with
milk)
2 eggs, beaten
1 teaspoon ground cinnamon
1 teaspoon vanilla extract (see p. 224)

Icing:
8 tablespoons butter
2 ounces unsweetened chocolate
6 tablespoons milk
1 pound powdered sugar
1 teaspoon vanilla extract
½ cup chopped pecans

Preheat oven to 350°.

Combine butter, oil, chocolate, and water in saucepan; heat until chocolate melts.

Combine flour, baking soda, sugar, sour
milk, eggs, cinnamon, and vanilla extract in
large bowl; blend with chocolate mixture.
Pour batter into greased 12 × 18–inch
sheet cake pan. Bake 20 to 25 minutes or
until cake is done. Frost with Mexican
chocolate icing.

To make icing: Combine butter, chocolate, and milk in saucepan; heat until bubbles form around edge. Remove from heat.
Add powdered sugar, a little at a time. Beat
well. Add vanilla extract and pecans. Beat.
Ice cake while still warm.

Lemonade

YIELDS 2½ QUARTS

1 cup superfine sugar
1 cup water
1⅓ cups fresh lemon juice
Finely grated zest of 4 lemons
2 quarts cold water
Ice cubes or crushed ice
Lemon slices and fresh mint leaves for
garnish

Combine sugar and water in small saucepan over medium heat; bring to boil. Reduce heat; simmer 5 to 6 minutes, stirring
occasionally. Remove from heat; cool completely. Combine syrup, juice, and zest in
large pitcher. Add cold water; stir well.
When ready to serve, fill tall glasses with
ice. Pour lemonade over ice and garnish
with lemon slices and mint.

Impatiens in South Garden

Summer Menus

George I Ewer, ca. 1725
Silver, Paul de Lamerie
Lent by Dr. George Heyer

WEDDING ANNIVERSARY CELEBRATION DINNER

for Twelve

* Shrimp Horcher

* Veal à la Marshall

* Citrus Carrots

Steamed Tiny New Potatoes with Parslied Butter

Romaine Salad Vinaigrette (see p. 225)

* Poached Peaches in Raspberry Sauce

Napa Valley Pinot Chardonnay, Private Reserve

June is the traditional month for weddings, and anniversaries must eventually follow. Whether it is your own, friends', or family members', celebrate. True, the veal is not a do-ahead entrée, but it is easy to prepare as well as being simply delicious. An important occasion warrants this special care. It may be browned and set aside to cool. Just before serving, return to skillet with the hot sauce and proceed with the recipe. The rest is virtually carefree.

Shrimp Horcher

SERVES 12

2 pounds boiled shrimp (see p. 100), deveined
6 ripe avocados, peeled and sliced
1 small jar red caviar

Sauce:
3 egg yolks
2 teaspoons dry mustard
6 tablespoons cognac
6 tablespoons chili sauce
¼ cup white wine vinegar
2 tablespoons lemon juice
½ teaspoon salt
¼ teaspoon ground white pepper
1 cup olive oil, divided
2 tablespoons finely chopped celery
2 tablespoons grated horseradish
2 tablespoons finely chopped shallots
2 tablespoons finely chopped parsley

Combine egg yolks, mustard, cognac, chili sauce, vinegar, lemon juice, salt, and pepper in blender or processor with 2 tablespoons oil. Blend. Make mayonnaise by adding remainder of oil in a slow stream. Add celery, horseradish, and shallots; mix thoroughly. Adjust seasoning to taste.

Arrange avocado slices and shrimp in attractive pattern on platter or on individual plates. Spoon sauce over. Decorate with ¼ teaspoon red caviar and parsley. Additional sauce can be passed.

Veal à la Marshall

SERVES 12

3 pounds veal, ¼ inch thick, cut into 12 large scallops or 24 small scallops
1½ teaspoons salt
½ teaspoon ground black pepper
6 tablespoons flour
6 tablespoons olive oil
8 tablespoons butter, divided
1½ cups beef consommé, divided
12 paper-thin lemon slices
2 tablespoons lemon juice

Dredge veal with salt, pepper, and flour; remove excess.

In large heavy skillet heat oil with 4 tablespoons butter over moderate heat. When foam subsides, add veal, only 4 or 5 pieces at a time. Sauté each side 2 minutes or until golden brown. Transfer with tongs to warm plate.

Pour off almost all fat from skillet, leaving thin film on bottom. Add ¾ cup consommé; boil briskly 1 to 2 minutes, stirring constantly and scraping in brown bits.

Return veal to skillet. Arrange lemon slices on top. Cover and simmer over low heat additional 5 to 8 minutes. Transfer to heated platter. Surround veal with lemon slices.

Add remaining consommé to skillet. Boil briskly until reduced to syrupy glaze. Add lemon juice; cook, stirring 1 minute. Remove skillet from heat. Stir in 4 tablespoons butter; pour over meat.

Note: For this amount, two skillets may be used.

Citrus Carrots

SERVES 12

48   baby carrots, 2 to 4 inches long
2   cups water
2   teaspoons salt
2   tablespoons butter
¾   cup fresh lemon juice
½   cup honey
½   cup cognac
½   cup Triple Sec or Cointreau
½   teaspoon salt
Parsley for garnish

Preheat oven to 350°.
Cook carrots in water with salt until barely tender. Drain. Place carrots in buttered baking dish and dot with butter.
Make syrup of lemon juice, honey, cognac, liqueur, and salt. Bring to boil. Pour over carrots. Bake 20 minutes, basting several times. Garnish with parsley.

Poached Peaches in Raspberry Sauce

SERVES 12

2   10-ounce packages frozen raspberries in heavy syrup
½   cup water
4   tablespoons sugar
12   peaches, peeled (halved and pitted, if desired)
2   tablespoons peach brandy
2   teaspoons Kirsch

Strain thawed raspberries through fine sieve into saucepan. Add water; bring to boil. Add sugar. Put peaches one at a time into sauce; let stand 2 minutes, spooning hot sauce over top of peaches. Place peaches into serving dish.
Bring sauce to boil for 2 minutes. Remove from heat and cool. Add brandy and Kirsch to sauce. Pour over peaches. Refrigerate several hours or until chilled.

Variation: Nectarines may be substituted for peaches.

Pepper No. 30, *1930*
Photograph by Edward Weston
Modern print by Cole Weston
Museum purchase with funds provided by Mr. and Mrs. Alvin S. Romansky

64

MEXICAN FIESTA SUPPER

for Eight

＊White Sangria

＊Yucatán Tortilla Soup

＊Pollo Pibil (Chicken Roasted with Achiote in Banana Leaves)

＊Budin de Pimiénto (Pepper Pudding)

＊Ensalada de Albaniles (Bricklayers' Salad)

＊Caramel Ice Cream

White Sangria

SERVES 8

1   fifth dry chablis
½   cup Cointreau
4   limes, thinly sliced
8   small bunches green seedless grapes
    (about 2 cups)
1   fifth champagne, chilled
Ice ring (optional)

Combine chablis, Cointreau, and sliced limes in pitcher. Chill thoroughly. Pour into punch bowl. Add grapes, champagne, and ice ring, if desired, or serve in pitcher.

Yucatán Tortilla Soup

YIELDS 3 TO 3½ QUARTS

1   chicken (3 to 4 pounds)
4   cups dry white wine
6   cups water
2   carrots, chopped (about 1 cup)
1   medium onion, quartered (about ½ cup)
6   sprigs parsley
4   sage leaves or ⅛ teaspoon dried sage
4   1½-inch sprigs fresh oregano or ⅛ tea-
     spoon dried oregano
6   1½-inch sprigs fresh thyme or ⅛ tea-
     spoon dried thyme
8   peppercorns
5   whole cloves
1   clove garlic
1   large onion, chopped (about 1 cup)
½   cup plus 1 tablespoon vegetable oil,
     divided
1   14½-ounce can tomatoes, chopped, with
     juice
1   teaspoon dried oregano
2   cubes or 2 teaspoons chicken base
     (optional)
2   tablespoons lime juice
Rind from one lime
1   teaspoon salt
⅛   teaspoon Tabasco sauce
6   corn tortillas
Chopped cilantro (optional)

Garnish:
3 ⅛-inch slices cream cheese per bowl or
    1 tablespoon sour cream and 1 table-
    spoon coarsely shredded Monterey Jack
    cheese

Simmer chicken in wine, water, carrots, onion, parsley, sage, oregano, thyme, peppercorns, cloves, and garlic until tender, about 45 minutes. Remove chicken from broth and bone, dicarding skin. Set aside. Return bones to broth and simmer 1 hour. Strain and return broth to stock pot.
Sauté large onion in 1 tablespoon oil. Add tomatoes with juice and additional oregano. Cook over low heat 5 minutes. Add to broth. Add chicken base, lime juice, rind, salt, and Tabasco sauce. Simmer. Remove rind after 5 minutes. Taste and adjust seasonings. Cut chicken into ¼-inch pieces and return to broth.

Cut tortillas into ⅜-inch strips, allowing ½ tortilla per serving. Fry in remaining oil until crisp (about ½ minute). Put fried tortillas in bowls; ladle in soup. Add chopped cilantro and top with cheese garnish.

Pollo Pibil
(Chicken Roasted with Achiote in Banana Leaves)

SERVES 8

⅔   **cup fresh lemon juice**
⅔   **cup fresh orange juice**
¼   **teaspoon salt**
24   **peppercorns**
8   **cloves garlic**
2   **tablespoons annato (achiote)** *
¼   **teaspoon dried oregano**
½   **teaspoon ground cumin**
2   **fresh chickens (about 3½ pounds each), cut into pieces**
Foil
Banana leaves * *

Place juices and all seasonings in blender or processor; purée until smooth.

Place chicken pieces in shallow, non-metallic dish. Cover with marinade, rubbing each piece well. Refrigerate 24 hours, turning once or twice.

Line flat pan with foil. Place chicken pieces with marinade in pan; cover with banana leaves. Seal with foil. Place in domed smoker with mesquite wood and pan of water. Smoke about 3 hours. Chicken may also be cooked in foil in 325° oven about 2½ hours. Serve with hot tortillas.

*The annato (achiote) must be covered with a little water and simmered about 5 minutes. Allow to soak at least 2 hours (overnight preferably) before grinding. Available at specialty shops.

**Banana leaves must be washed, dried, and then passed over a flame (about 6 inches above heat) to make them pliable.

Budin de Pimiénto
(Pepper Pudding)

SERVES 8

Vegetable oil (Mexican cuisine uses lard)
14   **stale corn tortillas, cut into 5-inch strips**
1   **large white onion, thinly sliced (about 1 cup)**
4   **large tomatoes, halved, broiled, and skinned**
2   **cloves garlic, peeled**
1   **teaspoon salt or to taste**
8   **red peppers, peeled, seeded, and cut into strips (or 8 chilies poblanos)**
8   **ounces crumbled queso fresco (or farmer cheese)**
1   **cup crème fraîche (see p. 222) plus 1 cup for garnish**

Heat oil in skillet to depth of about ¾ inch. Fry tortilla strips until they begin to stiffen but are not crisp. Remove with slotted spoon and drain well. Discard all but 3 tablespoons oil. Add onion. Fry until soft.

Meanwhile, blend tomatoes, garlic, and salt until smooth. Add to onions. Cook over fairly high flame about 3 minutes to thicken, stirring constantly.

Preheat oven to 375°.

In 9 × 14 × 2–inch dish, spread ⅓ of tortilla strips. Cover with ½ of pepper strips, ½ of cheese, and ⅓ of sauce, spreading thin layer of crème fraîche between each layer. Repeat and finish with tortillas and sauce. Cover with foil and bake about 20 minutes. Serve each portion with bit of crème fraîche.

Ensalada de Albaniles
(Bricklayers' Salad)

SERVES 8

2   chilies serranos
3   tablespoons finely chopped white onion
1   clove garlic, peeled
4 to 5 sprigs cilantro
1   cup tomatillos, blanched and drained
½   teaspoon salt
⅛   teaspoon sugar
⅓   cup water
⅓   cup finely chopped cilantro
2   avocados, thinly sliced
10 ounces queso fresco (or farmer cheese)
    or mozzarella, cut into strips

Combine chilies, onion, garlic, cilantro, tomatillos, salt, and sugar in blender or processor. Blend but do not overliquefy; sauce should have some texture. Stir in water and additional cilantro.

Place sauce in shallow dish or *molcajete*. Top with slices of avocado and cheese, garnished with few sprigs of cilantro. Serve with heated tortillas. (Each diner places slice of avocado and cheese, some chopped cilantro, and sauce on tortilla and rolls it up for easy eating.)

Caramel Ice Cream

YIELDS 2 QUARTS

3   cups cream
3   cups half-and-half
⅛   teaspoon salt
1   vanilla bean
12 egg yolks
1   cup sugar
6   tablespoons butter
2   cups sugar
2   cups water, divided

Combine cream, half-and-half, salt, and vanilla bean in large saucepan. Bring just to boil. Turn off heat. Cover and let steep at least 15 minutes.

Beat egg yolks and sugar until thickened and lemon colored. Stir part of hot cream into eggs. Slowly add remaining egg-sugar mixture to rest of hot cream. Cook over medium heat, stirring until mixture thickens slightly.

Remove from heat and stir in butter, piece by piece. Cool and refrigerate at least 4 hours or up to 3 days. Remove vanilla bean before using.

Combine sugar and ⅔ cup water in small saucepan; bring to boil. Cook, stirring constantly, until it caramelizes and turns dark tea color. Remove from heat. Slowly add remaining water. Cool to room temperature.

Add syrup to cream mixture. Transfer to ice cream mixer; freeze according to manufacturer's directions.

POOLSIDE LUNCH

for Six

* Iced Tomato-Orange Soup

* Curried Chicken-Shrimp Mold with Fruit Garnish

* Banana Bread Madame Hélène

* Cold Spiced Tea

Birdstone, ca. 2500 – 1500 B.C.
Unknown North American Indian
McDannald Collection

Iced Tomato-Orange Soup

YIELDS 1¾ QUARTS

3   cups chicken stock (see p. 221)
1   pound fully ripe tomatoes, cut into
     quarters
1   large carrot, chopped (about ½ cup)
1   medium onion, chopped (about ½ cup)
1   bay leaf
1   peppercorn
3½   tablespoons tomato paste
¼   teaspoon salt
¼   teaspoon sugar
3   tablespoons butter
3   tablespoons flour
1   cup heavy cream
3   tablespoons plus 1 teaspoon frozen or-
     ange concentrate, thawed
Strips of orange zest blanched for garnish

Put first nine ingredients into 3-quart
stainless steel or enamel saucepan. Cover;
simmer until vegetables are very soft (about
1 hour). Put through sieve, mashing to
force through as much vegetable pulp as
possible.

Melt butter; add flour and bring to simmer for 2 minutes, stirring constantly. Add
vegetable stock; cook over low heat, stirring until thickened.

Remove from heat; cool to room temperature. Add cream and orange concentrate; mix well. Chill thoroughly. Serve cold
garnished with strips of orange zest.

Curried Chicken-Shrimp Mold with Fruit Garnish

SERVES 6

2   envelopes unflavored gelatin
1½   cups chicken broth (see p. 221), divided
1   teaspoon curry powder
½   teaspoon salt
2   tablespoons lemon juice
1   cup sour cream
1   cup plus 1 tablespoon mayonnaise (see
     p. 223), divided
1   cup cubed cooked chicken
1   cup cubed cooked shrimp (see p. 100)
½   cup cubed avocado
¾   cup sliced toasted almonds
Lettuce, pineapple, grapefruit, mangos, kiwi,
     or papaya for garnish

Soften gelatin in ¼ cup broth. Set aside.
Heat remaining broth with curry powder
and salt. Add gelatin; stir until completely
dissolved. Stir in lemon juice. Cool in refrigerator until slightly thickened.

Stir in sour cream and 1 cup mayonnaise.
Fold in chicken, shrimp, avocado, and almonds. Spoon mixture into 6-cup mold or
individual molds, rubbed with remaining
mayonnaise. Chill until firm (4 to 6 hours).

Remove from molds, garnish with lettuce and fruit.

Banana Bread Madame Hélène

YIELDS 2 MEDIUM LOAVES

2¼ cups sugar
12 tablespoons butter
3 eggs
1½ teaspoons vanilla extract (see p. 224)
Zest of 1 lemon, grated
4 bananas, mashed (about 1½ cups)
3 cups flour
1 teaspoon baking soda
1 teaspoon baking powder
¾ teaspoon salt
⅓ cup sour cream
1 cup chopped nuts (optional)

Preheat oven to 350°.

Cream sugar and butter until light and fluffy. Add eggs, one at a time. Beat well. Add vanilla extract, zest, and bananas; mix well.

Sift together flour, baking soda, baking powder, and salt. Add sifted ingredients alternately with sour cream to mixture, mixing well after each addition. Blend in chopped nuts.

Butter and sugar two 9 × 5 × 3–inch pans. Divide batter between them. Bake in oven 30 to 40 minutes or until tester inserted in center comes out clean. Cool slightly in pans. Turn out on racks to cool.

Cold Spiced Tea

YIELDS 2 QUARTS

1½ quarts boiling water
6 teaspoons tea leaves
8 whole cloves
1 stick cinnamon, 3 inches long
½ cup sugar
1 large orange
1 large lemon
2 cups cold water

Pour boiling water over tea, cloves, cinnamon, and sugar.

Quarter orange and lemon and squeeze juice into tea mixture. Drop in rinds. Cover; steep 30 minutes. Uncover; add cold water.

SUMMER DINNER WITH OLD FRIENDS

for Four

*Cold Cantaloupe Soup

*Sweet-and-Sour Chicken

Steamed Broccoli with Browned Butter

Green Rice (see p. 27)

*Blue Cheese Surprise with Assorted Biscuits

Untitled, 1975
Photograph by Ralph Gibson
Anonymous gift

Cold Cantaloupe Soup

YIELDS 3½ CUPS

1   large cantaloupe, cut into 1-inch pieces
Juice of 2 limes
1   teaspoon honey
1   tablespoon frozen orange juice
    concentrate
¾ to 1 cup half-and-half
Mint leaves or sliced fresh strawberries for
    garnish

Peel, seed, and cut up cantaloupe. Purée in blender or processor. Add lime juice, honey, and orange juice concentrate. Blend until smooth.

Measure purée; use ⅓ the amount of half-and-half as purée. Stir until blended. Serve chilled with desired garnish.

Sweet-and-Sour Chicken

SERVES 4

1   fryer (2½ to 3 pounds), cut into serving
    pieces
½   teaspoon poultry seasoning
1   teaspoon salt
½   teaspoon ground pepper
¼   teaspoon paprika
4   tablespoons shortening
1¼ cups water
1   medium onion, finely chopped (about ¾
    cup)
3   tablespoons butter
1   tablespoon lemon juice
5   oranges, peeled and segmented
¼   cup vinegar
⅓   cup sugar

Wash and dry chicken. Sprinkle with poultry seasoning, salt, pepper, and paprika. Sauté chicken in shortening until golden. Add water; simmer 25 minutes. Set aside.

In small saucepan sauté onion in butter; add lemon juice. Remove from heat. Place oranges in pan. Mix vinegar and sugar; add to oranges. Simmer 15 minutes.

Arrange onions and oranges with sauce on chicken. Simmer 15 minutes or until tender. Serve on rice.

Blue Cheese Surprise

1 to 1½ pounds blue cheese
10 ounces raspberry preserves, either seed-
    less or strained
Melba toast and assorted biscuits

Place block of cheese on plate. Spread preserves over entire surface so that each portion sliced off will have a touch of the sweet taste on it.

Tybee Forks and Starts (H), *1978*
Photograph by Jan Groover
Gift of American Telephone and Telegraph Company

FOURTH OF JULY PATIO DINNER

for Eight

∗ Curried Clam Spread

∗ Jicama Salad

∗ Barbecued Brisket

∗ Fried Fresh Corn

∗ Baked Cherry Tomatoes

Fresh Fruit or Watermelon and Cookies

Beer or Wine

Curried Clam Spread

SERVES 8

⅓   cup vegetable oil
½   teaspoon mustard seed
2   tablespoons curry powder
2   bunches scallions, including tops, finely
     chopped
3   6½-ounce cans minced clams, drained
½   teaspoon salt

Heat oil in heavy skillet. Add mustard seed; cook over medium heat, stirring until seeds pop. Add curry powder; blend. Add scallions, clams, and salt. Heat thoroughly. Serve with Melba toast or wheat crackers.

Jicama Salad

SERVES 8

3 to 4 cups peeled jicama, cut into strips
1   green bell pepper, seeded and cut into
     strips
5   scallions, thinly sliced
1   large cucumber, cut into strips (about
     1½ cups)
¼   cup olive oil
½   teaspoon salt
½   teaspoon ground white pepper
1   teaspoon dried oregano
2   tablespoons white vinegar
¼   cup olive oil
¼   cup vegetable oil

Combine jicama, green pepper, scallions, and cucumber. Combine remaining ingredients. Pour over vegetables. Taste to correct seasoning. May be made 6 to 8 hours ahead.

Barbecued Brisket

SERVES 8 TO 10

1   beef brisket (4 to 5 pounds), trimmed
3   ounces liquid smoke
1   cup water
1   15-ounce can tomato sauce
¼   cup brown sugar
2   tablespoons Worcestershire sauce
¼ to ½ teaspoon Tabasco sauce
½   teaspoon salt

Preheat oven to 350°.
Place brisket in shallow roasting pan. Sprinkle with liquid smoke. Pour water around meat. Bake 2 hours.
Mix remaining ingredients in small saucepan; bring to boil. Spoon over meat. Continue baking, basting occasionally, until meat is tender (about 3 hours). Meat will look charred but will be tender and juicy inside. Slice thinly on diagonal to serve.

Fried Fresh Corn

SERVES 8

8 ears fresh corn
6 tablespoons butter
1 small onion, finely chopped (about ½ cup)
½ teaspoon salt
¼ teaspoon ground white pepper
2 teaspoons sugar
1 cup light cream

Cut kernels from corn. (There should be 4½ to 5 cups.)

In large skillet heat butter. Add corn, onion, salt, pepper, and sugar. Sauté 7 to 8 minutes. Stir often.

Remove from heat. Stir in cream. Return to low heat until just heated through. Do not boil.

Baked Cherry Tomatoes

SERVES 8

1½ boxes cherry tomatoes (about 1½ pounds)
¾ cup bread crumbs
⅓ cup Parmesan cheese
⅓ teaspoon salt
¼ teaspoon ground pepper
1½ teaspoons chopped fresh basil or ⅓ teaspoon dried basil
¾ teaspoon lemon-pepper marinade
3 tablespoons olive oil

Preheat oven to 350°.

Wash tomatoes and remove stems. Dry thoroughly; slice in half. Place in slightly oiled 13 × 9 × 2–inch oven-proof glass dish. Set aside.

Mix crumbs, cheese, salt, pepper, basil, and lemon-pepper marinade thoroughly. Add oil to moisten crumb mixture. Sprinkle over tomatoes. Bake uncovered 15 minutes.

Variation: Very small tomatoes may be cooked whole. Place closely together in 8-inch-square oven-proof glass dish.

Gloucester Harbor, *1938*
Oil painting by Stuart Davis
Agnes Cullen Arnold Endowment Fund

CRAB DINNER

for Six

* Red Pepper Soup

* Crab Meat with Black Butter

* Green Peas Sautéed with Jicama

* Meringues with Lime Bavarian

Chilled White Graves

Blue crabs in summer are plump and fat. The white nuggets of succulent meat are prepared here with a simple black butter sauce. Jicama—that crisp Mexican vegetable—is included to pick up the texture contrast with peas. Summer also brings sweet red peppers, featured in the first-course soup, and limes to give a refreshingly tart flavor to the Meringue Bavarian dessert.

Red Pepper Soup

YIELDS 1½ QUARTS

1   tablespoon butter
6   red bell peppers, seeded and cut into
    ½-inch pieces (about 4 cups)
2   large thinly sliced onions (about 2 cups)
2   cups double chicken stock (see p. 221)
2   cups sour cream
¼   teaspoon salt or to taste

Butter heavy saucepan. Place vegetables in pan. Cover with buttered wax paper and lid. Cook vegetables over low heat until tender (about 45 minutes).

Purée in food processor. Cool to room temperature. Add chicken stock, sour cream, and salt. Stir until smooth. Chill 2 to 4 hours.

Variation: For low-calorie version, substitute 4 cups buttermilk for chicken stock and sour cream.

Crab Meat with Black Butter

SERVES 6

2   pounds lump crab meat
Black butter
1   loaf French bread, sliced into ⅜-inch
    pieces, buttered and lightly toasted
Chopped parsley for garnish

    Black Butter:
1   pound butter
3   cloves garlic, split and each impaled on
    2 toothpicks
1   teaspoon dried tarragon
¼   teaspoon chopped fresh basil
3⅓ tablespoons lemon juice
2   teaspoons Worcestershire sauce
½   teaspoon salt
⅛   teaspoon Tabasco sauce (optional)
4   tablespoons finely chopped parsley

Melt butter over low heat in heavy stainless steel or enamel saucepan. Add garlic. Cook over low heat until golden brown (20 to 30 minutes). Stir to prevent particles from sticking. Add tarragon and basil. Continue to cook until dark brown, stirring constantly (about 5 minutes).

Remove from heat. Remove garlic. Add lemon juice, Worcestershire sauce, salt, Tabasco sauce, and parsley.

Sauce may be used immediately or refrigerated for a week. Reheat over water or immerse jar in hot water.

Drain excess fluid from crab; gently separate.

Heat black butter in saucepan over medium heat if made in advance. Add crab meat; toss gently to coat with sauce until heated thoroughly.

Serve crab meat on French bread. Garnish with parsley. Serve extra bread on the side.

Green Peas Sautéed with Jicama

SERVES 6 TO 8

1 medium jicama, cut into ⅜-inch cubes
   (about 1½ cups)
4 tablespoons butter
2 10-ounce packages frozen tiny green peas
   (about 3 cups)
¼ teaspoon salt
⅛ teaspoon freshly ground pepper

Drop jicama into boiling water for 1 minute. Drain.

Melt butter in saucepan. Add green peas. Stir until coated or until frozen peas are thawed. Add jicama and seasonings. Cook over medium heat, stirring until very hot (4 to 5 minutes). Serve immediately.

Meringues with Lime Bavarian

Meringues (YIELDS 8):

4 egg whites at room temperature
1 teaspoon lime juice
¾ cup minus 1 tablespoon extra fine granulated sugar (to beat in)
¼ cup minus 1 tablespoon extra fine granulated sugar (to fold in)

Lime Bavarian:
1 envelope unflavored gelatin
½ cup cold water
4 eggs, separated
1 cup extra fine granulated sugar
¼ teaspoon green coloring
½ cup (scant) lime juice
2 cups heavy cream

To make meringues: Preheat oven to 225°. Beat egg whites and lime juice to frothy stage. Continue beating and adding first amount of sugar 1 tablespoon at a time. When eggs almost reach stiff-peak stage, stop beating. Fold in second amount sugar.

Oil and lightly flour two baking sheets or cover with parchment paper. Draw eight 3-inch circles. Spoon meringue mixture into circles, forming rim around edge of each one. Bake 1 hour. Turn off heat. Open oven door; allow to cool about 10 minutes before removing from oven. When fully cooled, remove meringues from baking sheets. Store in air-tight container.

To make lime Bavarian: Mix gelatin and water. Place over hot water to dissolve. Remove; cool.

Beat egg yolks and sugar until pale and creamy. Add coloring. Stir in cooled gelatin. Add lime juice.

In separate bowl beat egg whites until stiff.

In another bowl whip cream to soft-peak stage.

Fold egg whites and cream into yolk mixture. Spoon Bavarian into individual molds or one large mold.

Unmold individual Bavarians onto meringues or spoon filling from large mold into meringues. For buffet service, large mold can be surrounded by meringues for guests to serve themselves.

The Little Sailboat, *1924*
Watercolor by John Marin
Bequest of Ida R. Nussbaum by exchange

SEA TROUT DINNER

for Eight

⁎ Iced Cucumber Soup

⁎ Sea Trout Baked with Ginger and Oranges

Buttered Rice

⁎ Watercress and Spinach Salad

with Sherry and Walnut Oil Dressing

⁎ Lemon Pie with Fresh Fruit

Chilled Muscadet

Iced Cucumber Soup

YIELDS 2 QUARTS

4   cucumbers, about 6 inches long
3   shallots or 1 medium onion, chopped (about ½ cup)
7   cups chicken stock (see p. 221)
2   tablespoons butter
2   tablespoons flour
¾   teaspoon salt
¼   teaspoon ground white pepper
3   egg yolks
¾   cup heavy cream, divided
1   tablespoon chopped chives or mint for garnish

Peel and seed cucumbers; cut into ½-inch slices. In pan combine cucumbers, shallots or onion, and stock. Simmer 15 to 20 minutes or until soft. Purée in processor or blender.

In large pan melt butter; add flour. Cook until bubbly and straw colored, stirring constantly. Add cucumber-stock purée. Heat to simmer. Season and continue to simmer 5 minutes. Remove from heat.

Lightly beat egg yolks. Blend into ½ cup cream in bowl. Slowly beat 1 cup hot soup into mixture. Return to soup. Heat until mixture slightly thickens. Do not boil.

Cover with plastic wrap; chill about 6 hours. Whip remaining cream until stiff. Serve soup in chilled bowls. Garnish with whipped cream and chives or mint.

Sea Trout Baked with Ginger and Oranges

SERVES 8

1   sea trout or similar fish (4 to 4½ pounds)
3   lemons
1   teaspoon salt
½   teaspoon ground white pepper
1   cup freshly squeezed orange juice
3   small cloves garlic, pressed
2   tablespoons chopped fresh gingerroot
2   tablespoons olive oil
6   tablespoons finely chopped parsley or coriander, divided
2   teaspoons Hungarian paprika
1 to 2   green bell peppers, cut into rings (at least one ring for each serving)
1 to 2   medium onions, thinly sliced
½   medium orange, thinly sliced (at least one slice for each serving)

Wash fish; dry with paper towels. Squeeze two lemons and sprinkle juice inside and on both sides of fish. Season inside and outside with salt and pepper.

Combine orange juice, garlic, gingerroot, oil, 4 tablespoons parsley or coriander, and paprika in processor or blender. Blend until smooth.

Cut two vertical slashes on each side of fish. Place fish in shallow oven-to-table baking dish. Pour sauce over fish, coating cavity and both sides. Let stand 30 minutes.

Preheat oven to 350°.

Arrange pepper, onion, and orange slices over and around fish. Cover dish tightly with foil. Place in upper third of oven. Bake 1 hour or until fish is opaque but not dry when tested with fork. Garnish with lemon wedges and remaining parsley. Serve immediately.

Watercress and Spinach Salad with Sherry and Walnut Oil Dressing

SERVES 8

1   pound fresh spinach with stems re-
    moved, washed and dried
½   pound watercress with stems removed
½   cup toasted pine nuts
¼   cup very dry sherry
½   small clove garlic, pressed
½   teaspoon salt
½   teaspoon Dijon mustard
⅔   cup walnut oil

Combine spinach, watercress, and pine nuts. Toss together with dressing to just coat.

To make dressing: Combine sherry, garlic, salt, and mustard. Stir until salt dissolves. Add oil; blend until thoroughly mixed.

Lemon Pie with Fresh Fruit

SERVES 8

1   cup sugar
¼   cup flour
4   eggs
1   cup light corn syrup
4   teaspoons butter, melted and cooled
Juice from 3 lemons
Grated zest from 2 lemons
Unbaked 9-inch pie crust (see p. 254)
Strawberries or other fresh fruit for garnish

Preheat oven to 350°.
Sift sugar and flour together.
Beat eggs. Blend sugar-flour mixture into eggs until smooth. Add syrup, butter, lemon juice, and zest.
Pour into pie crust. Bake approximately 45 minutes. Cool. Serve with strawberries or other fresh fruit.

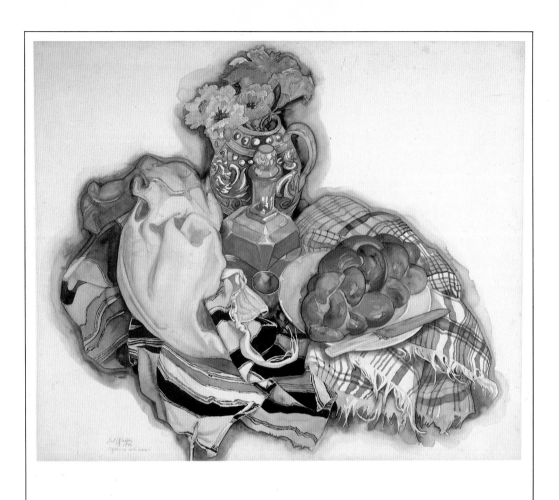

Blessing on Bread, *1936*
Watercolor by Saul Raskin
Gift of the Council of Jewish Women

CONCERT PICNIC AT ROUND TOP

for Ten

* Vichyssoise Verte

* Irish Soda Bread

Wedge of Bel Paese Cheese

Tea-Smoked Speckled Trout (see p. 245)

* Zucchini-Veal Moussaka

* Brandy Snaps

Fresh Fruits in a Basket

Thermos of Espresso

Chilled Beaujolais

The little town of Round Top (population 90) in Central Texas plays host to an inspiring music festival each summer for six weeks. From all over the state come the crowds each weekend. Under blue-black skies that glitter with millions of stars, the hillside facing the stage is dotted with picnic groups, some gathered around elaborate spreads, with silver, linens, and champagne, others with a traditional brown bag and a cooler of drinks. Serve this favorite menu on a colorful quilt with plump patchwork pillows to add to the comfort of the occasion. Make it a memorable evening.

Vichyssoise Verte

YIELDS 2 QUARTS

2   tablespoons butter
3   leeks, white part, sliced (about 2½ cups)
1   medium onion, sliced (about ⅔ cup)
2   tablespoons water
4   potatoes, peeled and sliced (about 1¼ pounds)
3   cups chicken broth (see p. 221)
2½ teaspoons salt or to taste
1   10-ounce package frozen spinach or fresh spinach, to make ¾ cup purée
2   cups half-and-half
½   teaspoon ground white pepper
⅛   teaspoon grated nutmeg

In large heavy saucepan melt butter; add leeks, onion, and water. Cover; cook over low heat until soft but not brown (about ½ hour). Add potatoes, broth, and salt. Cover; cook until potatoes are very tender.

Meanwhile cook spinach; drain well. Purée in blender or processor until very fine. Set aside.

When potatoes are tender, purée until very fine. Add spinach purée, half-and-half, pepper, and nutmeg. Cool to room temperature. Taste to correct seasonings. Chill overnight.

Irish Soda Bread

MAKES 1 LARGE OR 2 SMALL LOAVES

1   cup flour
2   cups stone-ground whole wheat flour
1   teaspoon baking soda
1   teaspoon salt
2   teaspoons baking powder
1   teaspoon sugar
4   tablespoons caraway, dill, or hulled sunflower seeds
1⅔ cups buttermilk

Preheat oven to 400°. Flour heavy baking sheet.

Mix together flours, baking soda, salt, baking powder, sugar, and seeds. Add buttermilk; mix thoroughly. Turn out onto floured board. With floured hands, knead lightly about 1 minute, adding more flour if necessary to keep dough from sticking to board.

Turn dough onto baking sheet in one of two ways:

1. Make large round loaf, cutting large X across center of loaf with floured sharp knife or razor.

2. Divide dough into two equal portions; form 2 elongated loaves. Place on floured sheet. Cut slashes diagonally across loaves at 2-inch intervals.

Bake 40 minutes or until loaves sound hollow when tapped on bottom. Large loaf may take 5 minutes longer.

Remove from oven; cool on rack. Crust becomes crisp when reheated 5 to 10 minutes before serving.

Zucchini-Veal Moussaka

YIELDS 6 SERVINGS

⅓ cup olive oil plus 2 tablespoons, divided
5 cups zucchini, cut into ⅓-inch slices
1 medium onion, finely chopped (about ½ cup)
2 garlic cloves, pressed
¾ pound ground veal
2 small tomatoes, peeled and chopped
1¾ teaspoons chopped fresh thyme or ¾ teaspoon dried thyme, divided
1½ teaspoons chopped fresh basil or ½ teaspoon dried basil
1 teaspoon salt or to taste
⅛ teaspoon pepper or to taste
2 eggs, beaten
4 ounces ricotta cheese
¼ cup grated Parmesan cheese
¼ cup chopped parsley
2 tablespoons breadcrumbs

Heat ⅓ cup olive oil in large skillet; sauté zucchini in batches until slightly brown. Drain; set aside.

Add remaining oil to same skillet; sauté onion and garlic 2 to 5 minutes. Add veal, tomatoes, ½ teaspoon thyme, basil, salt, and pepper. Cover; simmer on medium-low heat 15 minutes.

Preheat oven to 350°.

Mix eggs, cheeses, parsley, and remaining thyme. Set aside.

Oil 2-quart casserole; sprinkle with bread crumbs. Place layer of zucchini on bottom; cover with layer of meat. Continue alternating layers of zucchini and meat until all ingredients are used. Top with egg-cheese mixture. Bake 40 minutes. Broil 2 to 3 minutes until top browns. Serve at room temperature.

Brandy Snaps

YIELDS 6 DOZEN 2-INCH COOKIES

12 tablespoons butter
½ cup sugar
¼ cup dark brown sugar
½ cup dark molasses
⅜ teaspoon ground ginger
¾ teaspoon grated orange zest
¾ teaspoon ground cinnamon
⅛ teaspoon salt
1½ cups flour
1 tablespoon brandy

Preheat oven to 300°.

In saucepan melt butter; add sugars, molasses, ginger, orange zest, cinnamon, and salt. Cook until thoroughly blended and sugars are liquified. Remove from heat; add flour, stirring until smooth. Add brandy.

Drop by scant teaspoonfuls several inches apart on ungreased cookie sheet. Bake 10 to 12 minutes or until golden brown. Remove from oven and wait 2 minutes before carefully removing with spatula and placing on flat surface to cool.

The Rocks, *1888*
Oil painting by Vincent Van Gogh
John A. and Audrey Jones Beck Collection

90

SUMMER SUPPER

for Six

Cold Boiled Shrimp (see p. 100)

∗ Caviar Dressing

∗ Vegetarian Lasagna

∗ Blackberry Tart

Caviar Dressing

YIELDS 2½ CUPS

1 cup mayonnaise (see p. 223)
1 cup sour cream
3 to 5 drops Tabasco sauce
3 tablespoons lemon juice
¼ teaspoon ground white pepper
2 to 3 sprigs fresh dill, finely chopped, or
    1 teaspoon dried dill
3 scallions, very finely chopped
2 ounces lumpfish caviar (preferably
    Danish), carefully rinsed in very fine
    sieve
Cucumber slices and black caviar for garnish
    (optional)

Blend first 7 ingredients together. Carefully stir in caviar. Refrigerate overnight. Use as dip for raw vegetables or serve over cold shrimp* and hard-boiled eggs as salad or appetizer. Garnish with cucumber slices and black caviar if desired.

*3 pounds shelled, cooked shrimp (see p. 100).

Vegetarian Lasagna

SERVES 6 TO 8

1½ tablespoons vegetable oil or olive oil
1 large onion, chopped (about 1¼ cups)
1 large green bell pepper, chopped (about
    1 cup)
8 ounces fresh mushrooms, sliced
2 cloves garlic, pressed
1 15-ounce can tomato sauce
1 10-ounce can tomato purée
1 6-ounce can tomato paste
⅓ cup water (to rinse cans)
2¼ teaspoons salt
¾ teaspoon ground black pepper
3 tablespoons finely chopped oregano
    leaves or 1 tablespoon dried oregano
1½ tablespoons finely chopped parsley
1 teaspoon sugar
¾ cup sliced black pitted olives
3 tablespoons butter
2 eggs, well beaten
1 pound small-curd creamed cottage
    cheese
6 lasagna noodles
¾ pound mozzarella cheese, sliced
3 or 4 small zucchini, sliced lengthwise
¾ cup freshly grated Parmesan cheese

In 3½-quart heavy skillet or pot, heat oil. Sauté onion, green pepper, mushrooms, and garlic just until tender. Add tomato sauce, purée, and paste. Use water to remove last of sauces from cans; add to mixture. Blend. Bring to boil. Reduce heat to simmer. Add salt, pepper, oregano, parsley, and sugar. Simmer 15 to 20 minutes. Add olives and butter. Set aside.

In separate 4-to-6-cup mixing bowl, beat eggs. Stir in cottage cheese until blended. Set aside.

Cook noodles as directed on box, just until tender. Drain well.

Preheat oven to 375°.

Butter 13 × 9 × 2–inch glass baking dish. Layer as follows: ⅓ of sauce, 3 cooked noodles, ½ of mozzarella cheese slices, ½ of zucchini slices, ½ of cottage cheese and egg mixture. Repeat. Add remaining sauce. Top with grated Parmesan cheese. Bake 30 minutes. Let stand 10 minutes before serving. Freezes well.

Blackberry Tart

1 cup (scant) sugar
3 tablespoons tapioca
1 tablespoon grated orange zest
3 cups unsweetened blackberries, fresh or
   frozen
Pâté brisée for 9-inch tart (see p. 254)
2 tablespoons butter
2 tablespoons orange liqueur

Preheat oven to 375°.

Mix sugar with tapioca and orange zest. Mix with berries. (If using frozen berries, do not thaw.) Pour into 9-inch tart pan lined with pâté brisée. Dot with butter.

Bake 20 minutes. Lower heat to 325° and bake additional 25 to 30 minutes or until crust is browned. Remove from oven. Sprinkle orange liqueur over hot pie.

Variation: Boysenberries may be substituted.

LUNCH FOR TWO TABLES OF BRIDGE

for Eight

*Fresh Asparagus with Sauce

*Crab Soufflé

*Frozen Chocolate Almond Mousse

Chilled Chablis

The Turning Road, *1906*
Painting by André Derain
John A. and Audrey Jones Beck Collection

Fresh Asparagus with Sauce

SERVES 8

2½ pounds fresh asparagus or 3
10-ounce packages frozen asparagus

Sauce:
⅔ cup mayonnaise (see p. 223)
2 medium tomatoes, peeled, seeded, and chopped (about ⅔ cup)
1 tablespoon finely chopped fresh basil or ½ teaspoon dried basil or to taste

In small saucepan heat mayonnaise. Add chopped tomatoes and basil. Serve warm or cold with fresh asparagus or other fresh vegetables.

Crab Soufflé

SERVES 8

6 tablespoons butter
6 tablespoons flour
1⅔ cups milk
6 egg yolks
1 teaspoon salt
1 teaspoon dry mustard
¼ teaspoon (scant) grated nutmeg
¼ teaspoon Tabasco sauce (optional)
1½ cups grated Parmesan cheese, divided
1 pound crab meat
8 egg whites

Preheat oven to 425°.
Butter 8 individual 1-cup soufflé dishes or coquille shells.
Melt butter in saucepan; add flour. Cook, stirring constantly 2 minutes. Gradually add milk, stirring constantly over low heat until thickened and smooth.
Remove from heat; beat in egg yolks, one at a time. Add salt, mustard, nutmeg, Tabasco sauce, and 1 cup Parmesan cheese. Fold in crab meat.
Beat egg whites until stiff. Fold into crab mixture. Spoon into prepared dishes. Sprinkle each with remaining cheese.

Place dishes on cookie sheet. Bake in center of oven 10 minutes. Reduce heat to 400°; continue baking 5 to 10 minutes until top is golden brown and soufflés are very puffy. Serve at once.

Frozen Chocolate Almond Mousse

SERVES 10

⅓ cup chopped toasted almonds
½ cup crushed butter-flavored cookies
2 tablespoons sugar, divided
3 tablespoons melted butter
2 tablespoons Amaretto
2 cups vanilla ice cream, softened
2 eggs, separated
1 tablespoon rum
2 tablespoons strong coffee
6 ounces semisweet chocolate pieces, melted and cooled
½ cup whipping cream, whipped
Toasted almonds and additional whipped cream for garnish

Preheat oven to 350°.
Mix almonds, cookie crumbs, and 1 tablespoon sugar with melted butter. Press in bottom of 8-inch oiled springform pan. Bake 10 minutes. Cool; place in freezer.
Mix Amaretto and vanilla ice cream. Spread on crust; return to freezer.
Beat egg yolks until thick and lemon colored. Blend rum, coffee, and chocolate into eggs. Set aside.
Beat egg whites with remaining sugar until soft peaks form. Fold into chocolate mixture. Fold whipped cream into chocolate mixture. Spread over ice cream. Sprinkle with more almonds if desired. Freeze overnight. Garnish with whipped cream.

"DO AHEAD" LUNCH AT THE BEACH HOUSE

for Eight

Cold Sliced Tomatoes with Chopped Fresh Basil

⋆ Greek Fish Plaki

Greek Salad with Feta Cheese (see p. 135)

Crusty Loaves of Bread

⋆ Mango Ice Cream

Cold Beer

The Texas shoreline attracts thousands of sun worshippers each day during the hot weather, as any beach house owner can testify. Relaxed hospitality is the keynote as hot, thirsty, hungry guests return from a morning in the surf and sand. The unflappable hostess has simple and satisfying fare ready for the crowd.

Untitled, 1978 Photograph by Elliott Erwitt
Gift of American Telephone and Telegraph Company

Greek Fish Plaki

SERVES 8

⅓ cup olive oil
2 large onions, chopped (about 1½ cups)
2 cloves garlic, pressed
3 ribs celery, sliced ¼ inch thick (about 1½ cups)
3 carrots, peeled and sliced ¼ inch thick
1 pound tomatoes, sliced (about 4)
1½ pounds potatoes, sliced ¼ inch thick
3 teaspoons salt, divided
¾ teaspoon ground black pepper, divided
2 cups boiling water
3 pounds fish fillets
3 tablespoons lemon juice
½ cup sliced black olives
3 tablespoons chopped parsley

Preheat oven to 350°.

Heat olive oil in large casserole; sauté onions until golden brown. Add garlic, celery, carrots, tomatoes, potatoes, 1½ teaspoons salt, and ¼ teaspoon pepper. Add boiling water. Heat to boiling; cook over low heat 15 minutes.

Arrange fish over vegetables; add remaining salt and pepper and lemon juice. Cover; bake 10 minutes.

Remove cover. Add olives and parsley; cook additional 10 minutes.

Serve in shallow bowls with hot bread and a Greek salad flavored with lots of feta cheese.

Mango Ice Cream

YIELDS 4 QUARTS

1½ cups sugar
1 cup light corn syrup
2 teaspoons vanilla extract (see p. 224)
2 teaspoons almond extract
¼ teaspoon salt
2 cups heavy cream
2 cups light cream
4 cups fresh mango purée (about 4 large mangos)

In large bowl mix sugar, corn syrup, vanilla and almond extracts, and salt. Add creams; stir until smooth. Add mango purée. Pour mixture into ice cream freezer; freeze according to manufacturer's directions.

Fishing Boats, *1909*
Oil painting by Georges Braque
John A. and Audrey Jones Beck Collection

SEAFOOD BOIL

for Six

∗ Quiche with Character

∗ Cold Boiled Shrimp

∗ Cold Boiled Crab

∗ Red Sauce

∗ Remoulade Sauce

∗ Dilly Bean Salad

∗ Rich White Bread

Fresh Fruit and Cheese

Beer

Summertime along the Texas coast is made for lazy days and leisurely entertaining. One of the most popular meals is a "seafood boil," which includes Gulf Coast shellfish cooked, cracked, and piled high in the middle of newspaper-covered tables. Guests finish the job of picking meat from the shells and are provided with a variety of sauces in which to "dunk" it. With the addition of bread and a salad, it is as simple a meal as can be imagined. Add a quiche plus fruit and cheese and make it a party.

Quiche with Character

SERVES 6

Pâté brisée for 9-inch crust (see p. 254)
¾ cup grated sharp Cheddar cheese
½ cup grated Monterey Jack cheese
1 teaspoon chili powder
3 large eggs
½ cup cream
1 cup half-and-half
1 teaspoon salt
4 drops Tabasco sauce
1 4-ounce can diced green chilies
⅓ cup chopped ripe olives
1 tablespoon chopped scallions

Line pie plate with crust. Chill.
Preheat oven to 350°.

Mix cheeses together and spread on bottom of pastry shell. Sprinkle with chili powder.

Beat eggs slightly. Whisk in cream, half-and-half, salt, Tabasco sauce, chilies, olives, and scallions. Pour over cheese-covered pastry.

Bake 40 to 45 minutes or until knife inserted in center comes out clean. Serve hot or at room temperature.

Cold Boiled Shrimp

SERVES 6

6 quarts water
2 tablespoons salt
3 teaspoons pickling spice
4 bay leaves
8 black peppercorns
1 small onion, sliced
3 pounds shrimp in shells

Add seasonings to water and bring to boil. Add shrimp; cover and remove from heat. Leave shrimp in hot water 10 minutes; drain. Serve hot or cold.

Cold Boiled Crab

Allow 3 to 4 whole crabs per person

Drop crabs into large kettle of boiling salted water. Reduce heat and simmer 15 minutes. Remove from heat and cover. Leave crabs in hot water 10 minutes; drain. Serve cold.

Red Sauce

YIELDS 2½ CUPS

1 cup catsup
1 cup chili sauce
½ cup horseradish
4 tablespoons lemon juice
¼ teaspoon Tabasco sauce
1 tablespoon Worcestershire sauce
1 tablespoon angostura bitters (optional)
⅔ cup finely chopped celery
⅔ cup finely chopped scallions

Mix all ingredients together and chill at least 1 hour.

Remoulade Sauce

YIELDS 1⅓ CUPS

2   tablespoons cream-style horseradish
2   tablespoons finely chopped parsley
1   small onion, finely chopped (about ½ cup)
2   tablespoons finely chopped celery
¼   teaspoon Worcestershire sauce
2   tablespoons paprika
4   tablespoons Creole-style mustard
¾   cup vegetable oil

Mix together all ingredients except oil. Whisk in oil gradually to form emulsion. Chill.

Dilly Bean Salad

SERVES 6

2   10-ounce packages frozen whole green beans
2   cucumbers, peeled and thinly sliced (about 2 cups)
1   teaspoon salt

Dressing:
1   cup sour cream
1½ tablespoons dried dill weed
1½ teaspoons salt
1   tablespoon lemon juice
Ground white pepper to taste

Cook beans according to directions on package. Drain; refrigerate.

Sprinkle salt over cucumber slices. Drain in collander 1 hour. Rinse, pat dry, add to beans.

Mix all dressing ingredients together well. Toss with beans and cucumbers. Taste to correct seasonings.

Rich White Bread

YIELDS 2 LOAVES

2   cups warm water (110°)
1   package active dry yeast
8   tablespoons butter or margarine
⅓   cup sugar
1   teaspoon salt
6   cups flour, divided
3   eggs

Sprinkle yeast over water in mixing bowl. Add butter, sugar, salt, and 3 cups flour. Beat until smooth. Add eggs, one at a time, beating well after each addition. Add remaining flour; beat until smooth. Form into large ball. Place in clean bowl; wrap well with plastic wrap and refrigerate 12 to 18 hours.

Preheat oven to 350°.

Remove from refrigerator, punch down dough. Knead until all bubbles are removed. Divide into two parts. Shape into loaves.

Place in two 3½ × 8½–inch greased loaf pans. Cover; let rise again until doubled in bulk (about 1 hour).

Bake 45 minutes. Turn out of pans and cool on racks.

Artist's Brother in the Garden, *1878*
Oil painting by Gustave Caillebotte
John A. and Audrey Jones Beck Collection

for Eight

* Chilled Yellow Squash Soup

* Forty-Love Salad

* Tropical Ice

Wine and Beer

With its benign climate, most of Texas has tennis weather nine months of the year. Weekends often find family groups on the courts. Some enthusiasts organize their own tournaments with running competition from year to year. Those energetic souls are saluted with a menu for a cool lunch after the game.

Chilled Yellow Squash Soup

2½ pounds small yellow squash, sliced
1 small green bell pepper, sliced (about ½ cup)
1 large onion, sliced (about 1 cup)
4 cups chicken stock (see p. 221)
6 sprigs parsley
½ teaspoon dry dill weed
½ teaspoon salt
¼ teaspoon ground black pepper
2 cups sour cream

Put squash, green pepper, onion, and chicken stock in stainless steel or enamel pan. Simmer 20 minutes.

In processor or blender, purée mixture in batches. Add parsley, dill, and seasonings. Purée. Add sour cream; stir. Serve hot or chill several hours and serve cold.

Forty-Love Salad

SERVES 8

1 Bermuda onion, thinly sliced
1 cup boiling water
2 heads romaine lettuce, divided
3 whole poached chicken breasts, skinned and boned
6 ounces Monterey Jack cheese, cut into matchsticks
4 ounces hard salami, thinly sliced and quartered
½ cup ripe pitted olives
2 avocados, sliced
2 11-ounce cans mandarin orange sections, drained (optional)

Comino Dressing:
1 cup sour cream
1 cup mayonnaise (see p. 223)
4 tablespoons fresh lemon juice
½ teaspoon dry mustard
1 teaspoon comino (ground cumin)
8 tablespoons chili sauce

To make salad: Place onion slices in colander. Pour boiling water over; drain well; chill. Wash and dry romaine. Remove inner leaves from each head and chop coarsely.

Slice chicken into bite-size pieces. In large bowl toss chopped romaine, chicken, cheese, salami, olives, onion, avocados, and orange sections, if desired. Cover; chill until ready to serve.

To make dressing: Blend sour cream and mayonnaise. Add remaining ingredients. Chill. May be made day before serving.

To serve: Line individual plates with outer romaine leaves. Mound salad in center. Pass comino dressing, allowing guests to toss own salads.

Tropical Ice

YIELDS 5 CUPS (may be doubled for 8 servings)

2   cups sugar
4   cups water
2   cups puréed papaya
2   cups puréed mango
1   cup unsweetened pineapple juice
⅔   cup fresh lime juice
½   cup fresh lemon juice
¼   teaspoon salt
½   cup dark rum

Combine sugar and water; bring to boil. Boil 5 minutes. Cool. In processor or blender purée fruit. Add juices, salt, and rum; stir well. Mix in sugar syrup. Freeze in ice cream freezer according to manufacturer's directions.

The Seine at Paris, *1871*
Oil painting by Jean-Baptiste Armand Guillaumin
John A. and Audrey Jones Beck Collection

for Fifty

∗ Hot Tomato Bouillon

∗ Chilled Vegetable Platter with Water Chestnut Spread

∗ Smoked Fish Pâté

∗ Chicken Parmesan with Peanut Sauce

∗ Monterey Wontons with Guacamole Sauce

Assorted Cheese and Crackers

Fresh Strawberries and Pineapple Strips with Powdered Sugar

∗ Biscottini

Coffee

The cocktail party has come a long way from its original concept of cocktails plus a bowl of olives and one hot canapé. Today's hosts provide food in abundance. The menu is planned as a light meal around food that can be served with a minimum of formality. This party suggests a hot soup to be served in demitasse cups from a tureen on a side table. Guests help themselves. The table holds an assortment of spreads and "finger foods," with fruits, cookies, and coffee on a separate table.

Hot Tomato Bouillon

YIELDS 2 GALLONS (64 4-ounce servings)

Soup:
4 46-ounce cans tomato-vegetable juice
2 18-ounce cans tomato juice
10 10½-ounce cans beef bouillon
3 large onions, chopped (about 3 cups)
6 sprigs parsley
4 lemons, sliced
3 large bay leaves
18 peppercorns
Celery leaves from two ribs
1 teaspoon Tabasco sauce or to taste
Salt to taste
Sour cream and chives or dill to garnish

Simmer all ingredients except salt ½ hour. Remove from heat and let cool. Strain. Adjust seasonings. Serve with dollop of sour cream and chopped chives or dried or fresh chopped dill weed.

Chilled Vegetable Platter with Water Chestnut Spread

SERVES 50

6 pounds cherry tomatoes
8 pounds medium asparagus stalks, quickly blanched and drained
4 pounds yellow squash or zucchini, thinly sliced
4 pounds cucumber, peeled and cut into sticks
4 pounds carrots, peeled and cut into sticks
4 pounds celery, cut into sticks
4 pounds red bell peppers, cut into strips

Water Chestnut Spread (yields 2 quarts):
½ cup finely chopped fresh gingerroot
6 8-ounce cans water chestnuts, drained and finely chopped
3 pints sour cream
1½ cups finely chopped parsley
3 onions, finely chopped (about 1½ cups)
2 tablespoons soy sauce

Mix all ingredients together; chill at least 2 hours. Serve with crackers, as a fresh vegetable dip, or as filling for tea sandwiches.

Smoked Fish Pâté

YIELDS 10 CUPS

8   cups crumbled smoked kingfish, king mackerel, trout, redfish, salmon, or other fish (see p. 245)
1   pound butter
1   teaspoon freshly ground white pepper or to taste
1½ to 2 teaspoons anchovy paste or to taste
½   cup Dijon mustard or to taste
½ to ¾ cup heavy cream

Place fish and butter in small batches in processor or blender and process about 1 minute. Add pepper, anchovy paste, and mustard. Mix with ½ cup cream, adding more if necessary to achieve smooth consistency. Taste and correct seasonings. Mixture will be loose but will harden upon chilling. It also freezes well. Remove from refrigerator 15 minutes before serving.

Chicken Parmesan with Peanut Sauce

SERVES APPROXIMATELY 50 PERSONS AS HORS D'OEUVRE

18   whole chicken breasts, boned and skinned
3   pints fresh crumbs from French bread
3   pints fresh crumbs from pumpernickel bread
3   pints fresh crumbs from rye bread
3   pints freshly grated Parmesan cheese
3   tablespoons freshly ground black pepper
1½ dozen eggs, beaten with ¾ cup water
Oil for frying

Peanut Sauce (yields 5 cups):
Vegetable oil
3½ cups finely chopped scallions
8   large cloves garlic, pressed
6   red chiles japonés, seeded and finely chopped
¾   cup water, divided
4   cups crunchy-style peanut butter
1   cup orange juice
2   teaspoons ground cumin

Trim chicken and cut into diagonal strips ½ inch wide. Pound until very thin.

Mix all bread crumbs, cheese, and pepper together.

Dip chicken in egg mixture and then in breading mixture. Place on baking sheet until ready to fry.

In large, heavy skillet, pour 1 inch oil and heat until oil reaches 375°. Fry chicken pieces until golden brown; remove to paper towels to drain.

These are good served hot or at room temperature and hold well for several hours.

To make sauce: Wipe large saucepan with oil; add scallions, garlic, chiles, and ⅓ cup water. Cover and "sweat" on low heat until scallions are soft.

Combine mixture with remaining ingredients. Process in small batches until smooth. Serve warm or at room temperature.

Monterey Wontons
with Guacamole Sauce

YIELDS 160 WONTONS

Wontons:

2	pounds Monterey Jack cheese, grated
1⅓	cups drained and chopped canned mild green chili peppers
⅔	cup drained, seeded, and chopped canned jalapeño peppers
2	12-ounce packages wonton wrappers
4	cups vegetable oil for frying

Guacamole Sauce (yields approximately 2 quarts):

8	large ripe avocados, peeled, pitted, and coarsely chopped
3	cups chopped scallions
¾	cup lime juice
¾	cup mayonnaise (see p. 223)
2	teaspoons chopped fresh coriander
½	teaspoon ground coriander or to taste

Salt to taste

In bowl combine cheese, chili peppers, and jalapeño peppers, mixing well.

Arrange wonton wrapper with corner pointing toward you. Put 1 teaspoon filling in center of wrapper; fold bottom corner of wrapper over filling; fold in side corners to cover folded bottom corner. Moisten top corner of wrapper with water; roll wonton toward that corner, securely sealing point of wrapper. In same manner, continue to make wontons with remaining wrappers and filling.

Arrange filled wontons in layers in large pan, separating layers with wax paper. Seal and freeze.

When ready to serve, heat oil to 360° in deep fat fryer. Fry frozen wontons in batches 1 minute each or until golden. Drain on paper towels. Serve hot or at room temperature with guacamole dipping sauce.

To make sauce: In processor or blender purée avocados. Transfer to bowl; add scallions, lime juice, mayonnaise, coriander, and salt. Mix well; cover; refrigerate until ready to use.

Biscottini

YIELDS ABOUT 4 DOZEN

½	cup butter
1	cup sugar
3	eggs, room temperature
3	cups flour
3	teaspoons baking powder
½	teaspoon salt
1	teaspoon anise seed, crushed, or 1 teaspoon anise extract
1	cup ground toasted almonds

Preheat oven to 350°.

Cream butter and sugar until fluffy. Add eggs one at a time, beating well after each addition.

Sift together flour, baking powder, and salt. Add to sugar mixture in thirds, mixing well after each addition. Add anise seeds or extract and almonds. Turn onto lightly floured board and knead until smooth (1 or 2 minutes).

Divide dough in half, shape into 2 rolls, 15 inches long and 2 inches in diameter; bake 30 minutes on heavy cookie sheet or until firm to touch.

Remove from oven and immediately cut crosswise into slices about ¾ inch thick. Lay slices, cut side down, on cookie sheet; return to oven. Bake 20 to 30 minutes longer until completely dry and crisp. Flavor improves after 2 or 3 days. Keep well.

Millis Fountain with chrysanthemums
in Restaurant Garden
Photograph copyright by Gerald Moorhead

Axe Falls, *1981*
Acrylic and flashe on wood by Charles Arnoldi
Museum purchase in honor of William C. Agee with funds provided by William F. Stern,
Mr. and Mrs. Roy O'Connor, Mr. and Mrs. I. H. Kempner III, and Mr. and Mrs. Fayez Sarofim

FAMILY REUNION COOKOUT

for Twelve

⁎ Bloody Mary Punch

⁎ Chicken Ranch Style

⁎ Black-eyed Peas

Platter of Sliced Tomatoes and Purple Onions

⁎ 24-Hour Pickles

⁎ Crusty Stir Bread

⁎ Grand Prize Cookies

Iced Watermelon

Bloody Mary Punch

YIELDS 15 4-OUNCE SERVINGS

1½ quarts spicy tomato juice, chilled
1½ cups vodka
¼ cup freshly squeezed and strained lemon juice
1 tablespoon Tabasco sauce or to taste
¾ teaspoon celery salt
1 teaspoon Worcestershire sauce
Celery for garnish

Combine ingredients in punch bowl; mix well. Serve over ice cubes in highball glasses with celery.

Chicken Ranch Style

SERVES 12

3 frying chickens (about 3 pounds each), quartered

Basting Sauce:
½ cup white vinegar
1½ teaspoons Worcestershire sauce
3 teaspoons salt
2 tablespoons barbecue sauce
⅓ cup vegetable oil
3 tablespoons chopped white onion
6 drops Tabasco sauce
¼ teaspoon dry mustard

Prepare basting sauce 24 hours in advance. Mix all ingredients in small mixing bowl. Beat by hand until sauce is thoroughly blended. Refrigerate overnight.

Wash chicken and pat dry. Place chicken, skin side down, in 9 × 12–inch ovenproof dish. Cover chicken with prepared sauce; cover with foil. Refrigerate 8 hours.

Prepare good bed of coals on outdoor grill. When fire is ready, place chicken, skin side down, on grill. Baste and turn every 10 to 15 minutes. Cooking time will be 45 to 60 minutes.

Chicken may be served immediately or kept warm in 200° oven until serving time. If basted and covered while in oven, chicken will be moist and flavorful.

Black-eyed Peas

SERVES 12

4 pounds shelled fresh black-eyed peas
1 pound thick-sliced breakfast bacon cut into ¾-inch pieces
4 onions, finely chopped (about 2 cups)
4 large cloves garlic, finely chopped
Water to cover peas by 1 inch
4 tablespoons Worcestershire sauce
1 tablespoon plus 1 teaspoon salt
½ teaspoon Tabasco sauce

Rinse peas and pick over to clean.

Sauté bacon pieces in large pot until crisp; set aside.

Sauté onions and garlic in ½ cup bacon fat until soft but not browned. Add peas; stir. Cover with water by 1 inch. Cover. Simmer 1 hour, stirring and checking occasionally to see if additional water is needed.

Add Worcestershire sauce, salt, and Tabasco sauce. Simmer additional 30 minutes uncovered, stirring occasionally and checking moisture. Taste to correct seasoning. Add cooked bacon. (Cooking time for black-eyed peas varies with freshness and maturity. Late in the season they will take longer to cook and will absorb more water.)

24-Hour Pickles

YIELDS 4 QUARTS

10 large cucumbers, peeled and cut length-
    wise into quarters or sixths depending
    on size
1 2.87-ounce box mustard seed
1 ounce black peppercorns
2 medium onions, sliced (about 2 cups)
¾ cup fresh dill sprigs
4 to 6 bay leaves
1 cup white vinegar
2 cups water
1 cup sugar

In ceramic bowl or crock, layer cucumbers, mustard seed, peppercorns, onion, dill, and bay leaves.

Bring vinegar, water, and sugar to boil. Pour over cucumber mixture. Let stand under weight at least 12 to 16 hours. Pack into jars and keep refrigerated.

Crusty Stir Bread

YIELDS 2 MEDIUM LOAVES

4 cups flour
2 teaspoons salt
1 tablespoon sugar
1 package active dry yeast
2 cups water
½ cup butter, melted and cooled

Mix flour, salt, sugar, and yeast together well. Add water and stir until well blended. Cover and let rise approximately 3 hours.

Stir down well; divide between 2 8½ × 4½–inch well-buttered loaf pans. Let rise approximately 1 hour (leave enough room in tops of pans for butter).

Preheat oven to 400°.

Pour melted butter over tops of loaves. Bake 45 minutes or until top is brown and crusty.

Grand Prize Cookies

YIELDS 125 SMALL COOKIES

1 cup corn oil margarine
1 cup sugar
1 cup brown sugar
2 eggs
1 teaspoon vanilla extract (see p. 224)
2 cups flour
½ teaspoon salt
1 teaspoon baking powder
1⅔ teaspoons baking soda
2½ cups corn flakes
2 cups plus 2 tablespoons raw quick-cooking oatmeal
1 cup shredded packaged coconut
1 cup finely chopped nut meats (optional)

Preheat oven to 350°.

Cream margarine and sugars. Beat eggs and vanilla extract. Add to sugar mixture; mix thoroughly. Set aside.

Sift flour, salt, baking powder, and baking soda. Add to mixture. Fold in corn flakes, oatmeal, coconut, and optional nuts. Dough should be stiff and sticky. If not, add more corn flakes.

Lightly grease cookie sheet with vegetable oil. Make half-teaspoon cookies. Use second teaspoon to slide dough onto cookie sheet and round cookie dough. Bake 10 to 15 minutes.

After removing from oven, let cookies cool 1 minute. Then lift each one gently with spatula to prevent sticking. Leave cookies on sheet until cool and crisp.

The Marketplace at Pirna, *ca. 1750*
Painting by Bernardo Bellotto
Samuel H. Kress Collection

BEFORE THE SYMPHONY DINNER

for Six

⋆ Cream of Mushroom Soup

⋆ Baked Fish à la Grecque

Pasta with Cheese and Butter

Mixed Green Salad with Vinaigrette (see p. 225)

⋆ Wine-Baked Apples

Demestica or Pinot Grigio

Cream of Mushroom Soup

SERVES 6 TO 8

¼   pound butter or margarine
1   clove garlic, finely chopped
1   small onion, finely chopped (about ½ cup)
1   pound mushrooms, sliced
4   tablespoons flour
4   cups chicken broth (see p. 221)
1   teaspoon salt or to taste
¼   teaspoon ground pepper
2   tablespoons lemon juice
2   cups half-and-half

Melt butter in large saucepan. Sauté garlic and onion until translucent. Add mushrooms and cook until barely soft, stirring occasionally. Add flour and blend well.

Place vegetables in processor or blender with 1 to 2 cups broth. Blend to finely chopped stage—stop short of smooth.

Return to saucepan. Add remaining broth and heat to very hot but do not boil. Add salt, pepper, and lemon juice while heating. Add half-and-half and heat. Taste and adjust seasonings if needed.

Note: Low-fat milk may be used instead of half-and-half, but then increase flour to 6 tablespoons.

Baked Fish à la Grecque

SERVES 6

½   cup olive oil, divided
1   whole fish (4 to 5 pounds) or 4 pounds fish fillets (trout, redfish, etc.)
1   teaspoon salt, divided
½   teaspoon freshly ground pepper, divided
2   tablespoons lemon juice
1   lemon, sliced very thin
4   tomatoes, sliced (about 1 pound)
2   large onions, thinly sliced
2   tablespoons finely chopped parsley
3   teaspoons finely chopped fresh oregano or 1 teaspoon dried oregano
1   tablespoon finely chopped fresh thyme or ½ teaspoon dried thyme
1   large clove garlic, pressed
½   cup dry white wine
1   tablespoon dried black raisins (optional)

Preheat oven to 350°.

Brush with oil shallow pan large enough to hold fish in one layer.

Sprinkle fish with ½ teaspoon salt and ¼ teaspoon pepper. Sprinkle with lemon juice. Place fish in pan; cover with lemon slices. Place tomato and onion slices on and around fish. Sprinkle with chopped parsley, herbs, garlic, and remaining salt and pepper. Pour remaining olive oil, wine, and optional raisins around fish.

Bake whole fish 1 to 1¼ hours or fillets ¾ to 1 hour. Baste every 15 minutes. Bake until fish flakes easily with fork.

Wine-Baked Apples

SERVES 6

4   tablespoons butter
¼   cup golden raisins
2   teaspoons chopped candied lemon peel
⅔   cup brown sugar
6   large firm apples (such as Pippin), cored but not peeled
1½ cups dry white wine

Preheat oven to 350°.

Melt butter; add raisins, lemon peel, and sugar. Set aside.

Core apples, leaving thin section at bottom. Remove strip of peel from center of apple to prevent bursting during cooking. Place apples in baking dish. Divide mixture evenly; fill cavities. Add wine; bake 30 to 40 minutes until fruit is tender, basting occasionally.

Remove apples to serving dish. Pour juices into small saucepan. Cook over high heat until syrup forms. Spoon sauce over each apple.

Nature Morte, *1938*
Photograph by Florence Henri
Museum purchase with anonymous funds

TAILGATE PARTY

for Six

* Shrimp Dip

Carrot and Celery Sticks

* Empanadas Criollas (Argentine Meat Turnovers)

Apples, Grapes, Cheeses

* Sugared Texas Pecans

Football time—class reunion time—picnic time. Parking lots by the stadium begin to fill early as enthusiastic fans pull down the tailgate and set up campstools to enjoy a picnic before the game (to say nothing of getting a good parking place). Finger food is the rule here. Bright large napkins and plastic glasses, no plates or cutlery to bother with. Hearty red wine, beer, and a thermos of hot coffee complete the carefree meal.

Shrimp Dip

SERVES 6–8

2   pounds shrimp, cooked, cleaned, and coarsely chopped (see p. 100)

Dip:
2   cups salad dressing or mayonnaise (see p. 223)
2   8-ounce packages cream cheese, softened
1   medium onion, finely chopped (about ½ cup)
1   small green bell pepper, finely chopped (about ½ cup)
2   ribs celery, finely chopped (about ¾ cup)
½   teaspoon garlic salt
10 drops Tabasco sauce
1   teaspoon sugar
Juice of 1 lemon
½   teaspoon Cayenne pepper
½   teaspoon seasoned salt

Prepare day before serving. Blend salad dressing or mayonnaise with cream cheese. Add rest of ingredients. Refrigerate overnight. Just before serving add shrimp.

Empanadas Criollas
(Argentine Meat Turnovers)

SERVES 6

2   tablespoons butter or margarine
2   medium onions, finely chopped (about ¾ cup)
1   green bell pepper, finely chopped (about ⅔ cup)
1½ pounds ground meat
1   teaspoon salt
1   teaspoon paprika
1   teaspoon ground cumin
½   teaspoon Cayenne pepper or to taste
1   teaspoon sugar
2   hard-boiled eggs, finely chopped
½   cup golden raisins
12 large stuffed green olives, thinly sliced
1   17¼-ounce package frozen puff pastry

Preheat oven to 400°.
Melt butter in large skillet; sauté onion and green pepper. Remove.
Using same skillet brown meat. Add remaining ingredients, onion, and green pepper. Mix thoroughly.
Roll puff pastry as thin as pie crust. Using a 3- to 4-inch biscuit cutter, divide pastry into circles. Cover one-half circle with meat mixture; fold over. Crimp edges of pastry with fork. Continue process until all mixture is used.
Place on cookie sheet; bake 20 minutes or until brown. Pastry may be cut into any desired shapes or sizes and used small as hors d'oeuvre or large as entrée.

Sugared Texas Pecans

1   cup sugar
½   cup water
10   ounces pecan halves
½   teaspoon maple extract
½   teaspoon cinnamon

Combine sugar and water in heavy skillet. Cook 5 minutes. Add pecans; stir until syrup becomes white. Remove from heat; add maple extract and cinnamon. Cool 10 minutes.

Return skillet to low heat; stir until sugar starts to melt, being careful to keep halves unbroken. Pour onto waxed paper; separate nuts slightly. Allow to dry.

The Herd Boy, *1890*
Oil painting by Frederic Remington
Hogg Brothers Collection

AFTER THE GAME SUPPER

for Eighteen

⋆Easy Game Pâté

⋆Southern Gumbo

Rice

French Bread (see p. 143)

Relish Tray

⋆Buttermilk Sheet Cake with Praline Icing

Beaujolais

Easy Game Pâté

YIELDS 5 CUPS

2   pounds cleaned whole duck livers
6   tablespoons butter
2   tablespoons olive oil
⅔   cup Madeira
½   pound butter at room temperature
4   tablespoons lemon juice
2   teaspoons finely chopped fresh thyme or
    1 teaspoon dried thyme
2   teaspoons salt
1   teaspoon cracked pepper
Watercress and pimiento strips for garnish

Sauté livers in butter and oil until browned but still pink in center.

Heat Madeira; pour over livers. Flame. Place livers and pan juices in processor or blender; purée. Cool.

Add butter to cooled purée. Add lemon juice, thyme, salt, and pepper, blending until smooth. Taste to correct seasonings. Spread into decorative crock and chill. Garnish with watercress and pimiento strips. Serve with crackers or Melba toast.

Variation: Chicken livers may be substituted.

Southern Gumbo

SERVES 18 TO 24

1   cup cooking oil
1   cup flour
4   ribs celery, chopped
2   large onions, chopped (about 2 cups)
1   large green bell pepper, chopped
    (about 1 cup)
2   cloves garlic, finely chopped
½   cup chopped parsley (optional)
1   pound okra, sliced
2   tablespoons oil, additional
2   quarts chicken stock (see p. 221)
2   quarts water
½   cup Worcestershire sauce
1   large ripe tomato, chopped
¼   teaspoon Tabasco sauce
½   cup catsup
2   tablespoons salt
4   slices bacon, chopped
2   bay leaves
¼   teaspoon dried thyme
¼   teaspoon dried rosemary
⅛   teaspoon red pepper flakes (optional)
2   cups cooked chicken cut into ½-inch
    cubes
1   pound crab meat
1   pound crab fingers
4   pounds shrimp, cooked and cleaned
    (about 5½ pounds raw headless shrimp;
    see p. 100)
1   pint oysters (optional)
1   teaspoon brown sugar
3   tablespoons lemon juice (optional)

Heat oil in heavy pot over medium heat. Add flour slowly, stirring constantly with wooden spoon until roux is brown (will take 20 to 30 minutes).

Add celery, onion, green pepper, garlic, and parsley; simmer 45 minutes to 1 hour, stirring regularly to prevent sticking. (Cooking time may be cut at this point, but gumbo will not be the same.)

Fry okra in 2 tablespoons oil until brown and no longer stringy. Combine roux-vegetable mixture with okra in large stock pot and stir well over low heat. (At this point the mixture may be cooled, packaged, and frozen or refrigerated for later use.)

Add chicken stock, water, Worcestershire sauce, tomato, Tabasco sauce, catsup, salt, bacon, bay leaves, thyme, rosemary, and red pepper flakes. Simmer 2½ to 3 hours.

About 15 minutes before serving time, add cooked chicken, crab meat and fingers, and shrimp. If oysters are included, add them 5 minutes before serving. Just before serving, add brown sugar and lemon juice. Stir well; taste and correct seasoning if needed. Serve over cooked rice in soup bowls.

Note: Gumbo file spice may be added along with additional red pepper just before serving.

Buttermilk Sheet Cake with Praline Icing

SERVES 24

2	cups sugar
2	cups flour
8	tablespoons butter
8	tablespoons vegetable shortening
1	cup water
½	cup buttermilk
1	teaspoon vanilla extract (see p. 224)
2	eggs, slightly beaten
1	teaspoon baking soda

Praline Icing:

1½	cups brown sugar
1	cup sugar
3	tablespoons butter
1	cup cream
¾	cup chopped pecans
1½	teaspoons vanilla extract

Preheat oven to 400°.

Sift sugar and flour together. Set aside.

Melt butter and vegetable shortening together. Add water and bring to boil. Remove from heat. Beat into flour-sugar mixture. Add buttermilk, vanilla extract, eggs, and baking soda. Mix well and pour into buttered 11 × 17¾-inch pan. Bake 20 minutes. Remove from oven. Spread with praline icing.

To make icing: Combine sugars, butter, and cream in saucepan. Cook over medium heat to soft-ball stage (236°). Remove from heat and cool about 6 minutes. Add pecans and vanilla extract. May be thinned with cream if it seems too thick. Because icing may harden, score cake for slicing after spreading icing.

Flood on the Road to St. Germain, *1876*
Oil painting by Alfred Sisley
John A. and Audrey Jones Beck Collection

VEAL DINNER

for Eight

⋆ Shrimp Provençal
⋆ Veal Fricassee with Tarragon
Buttered Rice or Pasta
Endive Salad with French Dressing
⋆ Caramel-Pecan Cheesecake
Médoc or Other Light Bordeaux

Shrimp Provençal

SERVES 8

2   pounds large shrimp, boiled, shelled, and deveined (see p. 100)
1   lemon, thinly sliced
1   purple onion, thinly sliced
½   cup sliced and pitted black olives
2   tablespoons chopped pimiento
⅓   cup fresh lemon juice
1   tablespoon white wine vinegar
1   clove garlic, pressed
½   bay leaf, finely crumbled
1   tablespoon dry mustard
¼   teaspoon Cayenne pepper or to taste
1   teaspoon salt
½   teaspoon ground pepper
¼   cup olive oil
1   tablespoon capers
2   tablespoons finely chopped parsley
Parsley sprigs for garnish (optional)

Place shrimp in three-quart bowl with lemon, onion, olives, and pimiento. Mix well. Set aside.

Combine lemon juice, vinegar, and spices in small bowl. Add oil. Beat well. Stir dressing mixture into shrimp. Add capers and parsley. Cover. Refrigerate at least 2 hours before serving. Taste to adjust seasonings. Serve on individual plates garnished with sprigs of parsley.

Veal Fricassee with Tarragon

SERVES 6 TO 8

3   tablespoons butter
3   tablespoons olive oil
3   pounds veal shoulder roast, cut into 1-inch cubes
4   tablespoons flour
4   cups chicken broth (see p. 221)
1½   teaspoons salt
1   bay leaf
1   teaspoon chopped fresh thyme or ½ teaspoon dried thyme
½   teaspoon ground white pepper
2   large onions, peeled and quartered
3   tablespoons tarragon vinegar
2   tablespoons chopped fresh tarragon or 1 tablespoon dried tarragon
3   egg yolks
1   cup light cream
¼   cup chopped fresh parsley
½   cup vermouth or white wine (only if made ahead; see note)

Melt butter and oil in heavy saucepan over medium-high heat. When very hot, add meat and brown lightly on all sides. As liquid forms, drain off and save. When meat is browned, sprinkle with flour. Stir; cook over low heat 2 minutes. Gradually add chicken broth and juice from meat. Add salt, bay leaf, thyme, and pepper. Add onions. Cover tightly. Cook over very low heat 1¼ to 1½ hours or until meat is tender. Stir occasionally to prevent sticking. Do not overcook.

When meat is done, add vinegar and tarragon. Remove from heat. Gradually stir in beaten egg yolks mixed with cream. Return to low heat, stirring constantly. Heat but do not boil. Sprinkle with chopped parsley.

Note: May be made ahead and refrigerated overnight. On reheating, slowly stir in vermouth or white wine. Heat on very low heat, stirring often. Do not boil.

Caramel-Pecan Cheesecake

SERVES 8

Pecan Crust:
1¼ cups ground pecans
2 tablespoons sugar
¼ cup melted butter

Filling:
12 ounces cream cheese at room
    temperature
1 teaspoon vanilla extract (see p. 224)
½ cup sugar
2 large eggs
2 cups sour cream
⅛ teaspoon salt

Caramel Topping:
1¼ cups brown sugar
⅔ cup corn syrup
4 tablespoons boiling water
¾ cup half-and-half
1 cup pecan halves

Preheat oven to 350°.

To make crust: Place pecans, sugar, and butter in small bowl; stir until well blended. Press mixture in even layer into bottom of 9 × 3–inch spring pan. Set on center rack in oven. Bake 8 to 10 minutes until partially cooked. Remove from oven. Cool to room temperature. Lower rack to bottom third of oven. Meanwhile prepare filling.

To make filling: In large bowl beat cream cheese until very smooth. Add vanilla extract and sugar; beat well. Add eggs, one at a time, beating and scraping bowl occasionally with spatula. Beat until smooth after each addition. Add sour cream and salt; mix thoroughly. Beat until smooth.

Place filling in crust. Bake 30 minutes (it will appear soft, but it is done). Remove to rack and cool to room temperature. Refrigerate 5 to 6 hours before serving.

To make topping: Dissolve brown sugar in corn syrup and boiling water. Add half-and-half; mix well. Cook over moderate heat until thickened and very smooth. Cool and refrigerate. It will thicken when chilled.

When ready to serve, place pecan halves on top of cake. Warm caramel topping and pour over cake or serve in separate container.

Red Figure Hydria, ca. 470 B.C.
Greek ceramic vase
Museum purchase with funds provided by General and Mrs. Maurice Hirsch

GREEK FARE

for Eight

＊Avgolemono (Lemon Soup)

＊Leg of Lamb with Savory Sauce

＊Herbed Lemon Pilaf

＊Greek Salad

＊Orange Ice

Chilled White Mâcon or Hermitage

October brings the Greek Festival to Houston. At the Annunciation Greek Ortho-dox Cathedral food, wine, clothes, jewelry, dancing, and singing provide thousands of people an imaginary trip to the Aegean for a few hours. This Greek fare menu salutes those dedicated parishioners who prepare a great feast in the finest tradition.

Avgolemono
(Lemon Soup)

YIELDS 6 CUPS

1   chicken (3 to 4 pounds)
1   rib celery, cut into 1-inch pieces
1   bay leaf
1   onion studded with 2 cloves
1   carrot, cut into 1-inch pieces
1   tablespoon salt
Water to cover
1/3   cup rice
3   egg yolks
1   teaspoon cornstarch
1/2   teaspoon ground white pepper or to taste
3   tablespoons lemon juice or to taste

Place chicken, celery, bay leaf, onion, carrot, and salt in large saucepan. Barely cover with water; cover; simmer 1 to 2 hours or until tender.

When chicken is tender, remove and reserve chicken for another dish. Strain broth. Cool; remove all fat. Measure broth; either reduce to 6 cups or add water to increase to 6 cups. Pour broth in pan; add rice. Boil 20 minutes. Remove from heat.

Beat egg yolks. Add 1 cup broth to cornstarch, stirring constantly. Stir into egg yolks. Return liaison to broth. Cook over low heat until slightly thickened, stirring constantly. Do not boil. Add pepper and lemon juice. Let stand 5 minutes. Taste and adjust seasonings. Serve immediately.

Note: Double chicken stock (see p. 221) may be used in place of broth in recipe.

Leg of Lamb with Savory Sauce

SERVES 8

1   leg of lamb (5 pounds), boned, rolled, all fat removed
2   cloves garlic, slivered
1/4   teaspoon dried thyme
1/4   teaspoon dried rosemary
1/3   cup olive oil
1/4   cup chopped fresh basil or 1/4 teaspoon dried basil
1/2   teaspoon salt
1/8   teaspoon ground pepper

  Sauce:
1   tablespoon vegetable oil
3   tablespoons finely chopped shallots
1   medium tomato, peeled, seeded, and finely chopped
Drippings from lamb roast, fat removed
1/2   cup white wine
1/2   cup beef stock (see p. 220)
1/4   cup chopped fresh basil
1   tablespoon heavy cream

Preheat oven to 350°.

With sharp knife, make evenly spaced insertions in lamb; stuff with garlic slivers. Mix thyme and rosemary; rub into lamb. Coat meat with oil; sprinkle with basil, salt, and pepper. Roast 1 hour and 15 minutes for rare (125° for rare or 140° for well done on meat thermometer).

To make sauce: Heat oil in heavy skillet; add shallots. Cook until soft but not brown. Add tomato; mix well.

Deglaze roasting pan with wine and stock. Combine with shallot-tomato mixture. Add basil and cream; heat but do not boil.

Herbed Lemon Pilaf

SERVES 8

2   medium onions, chopped (about 1 cup)
4   tablespoons butter
2¾ cups chicken stock (see p. 221)
3   tablespoons lemon juice
Bouquet garni: 6 basil stems, ½ teaspoon
    dried thyme, and ½ bay leaf tied up in
    cheesecloth or garni bag
1   teaspoon salt
¼   teaspoon ground white pepper
2   cups long-grain rice
Blanched julienne lemon zest and basil
    flowers for garnish

Cook onion in butter over low heat until softened. Add chicken stock, lemon juice, and bouquet garni. Add salt and pepper. Bring liquid to boil; add rice. Stir. Cover; cook until rice is tender. Discard bouquet garni. Fluff rice. Garnish with lemon zest and basil flowers.

Greek Salad

SERVES 8 TO 10

2   heads romaine lettuce, using hearts only
2   medium onions, thinly sliced (about
    1½ cups)
1   cucumber, peeled and thinly sliced
2   green bell peppers, thinly sliced
10 to 12 Italian plum tomatoes, quartered
1   pound feta cheese, crumbled, or to taste
24 Greek olives or to taste
Vinegar and oil
Ground black pepper and salt to taste

Arrange lettuce on platter. Separate onion rings; place on greens. Add cucumber, green peppers, and tomatoes. Cover with cheese and olives. Sprinkle vinegar and oil over salad. Season with pepper and salt.

Orange Ice

YIELDS 3 PINTS

4   cups water
1½ cups sugar
2   cups orange juice
½   cup lemon juice
Grated zest of orange and fresh mint for gar-
    nish (optional)

In large saucepan, bring water and sugar to boil over moderate heat. Stir only until sugar dissolves. Cook mixture exactly 5 minutes, timing from moment sugar and water begin to boil. Immediately remove pan from heat; cool to room temperature.

Add orange and lemon juice. Stir. Pour into trays or shallow pan.

Cover and freeze 3 to 4 hours, stirring every 30 minutes. Serve in chilled sherbet dishes. Garnish with zest and/or mint if desired.

A GERMAN CELEBRATION DINNER

for Eight

∗ Cheese Pretzels

∗ Sauerbraten

∗ Kartoffelsalat (Hot German Potato Salad)

∗ Rotkohl (Braised Red Cabbage)

∗ Chocolate Sauerkraut Cake

Beer

"Oktoberfests" are traditional fall events in Central Texas towns where the descendants of early German settlers celebrate their heritage with traditional music, dancing, and feasting. It's an exuberant and happy occasion for all generations, from babies in strollers to great-grandparents. The menu that follows might be served at home on this special occasion as an alternative to the ubiquitous barbecue.

Cheese Pretzels

YIELDS ABOUT 32 PRETZELS

1   package active dry yeast
1½   cups warm water (110°)
1   tablespoon sugar
1   teaspoon salt
4   cups flour
2   cups grated extra sharp Cheddar cheese
1   egg
2   tablespoons coarse salt

Preheat oven to 425°.

Sprinkle yeast over warm water and stir to dissolve. Add sugar and salt. Add flour and cheese alternately, reserving 2 tablespoons flour in case dough sticks during kneading.

Knead dough until smooth and elastic. For crisp pretzels, cut into 32 pieces. Roll each piece into 7-inch rope; shape into pretzels, rings, or sticks.

Place on ungreased cookie sheet; brush with beaten egg and sprinkle with coarse salt. Bake 15 to 18 minutes.

For thicker, chewier pretzels, place dough in greased bowl and turn to coat completely. Cover; allow to rise until doubled in bulk. Punch down and shape as above. Cook immediately or allow to rise 10 to 20 minutes before baking.

Baked pretzels may be frozen and reheated in 300° oven for 5 minutes.

Sauerbraten

SERVES 8

2   cups vinegar
2   cups water
4   medium onions, sliced
2   ribs celery, chopped
2   carrots, chopped
3   bay leaves
8   peppercorns, crushed
8   whole cloves
¼   teaspoon mustard seeds
1   beef rump roast (4½ pounds)
1   teaspoon salt
¼   teaspoon ground pepper
¼   cup vegetable oil
¼   cup flour
½   cup seedless raisins, soaked in ½ cup hot water
½   cup sour cream

Combine first nine ingredients in saucepan. Bring to boil. Remove from heat and cool. Place meat in large bowl; pour marinade mixture over it. Refrigerate; marinate 2 to 3 days, turning several times.

Remove meat from marinade; pat dry. Sprinkle with salt and pepper.

Heat oil in heavy Dutch oven; brown meat well on all sides. Add 2 cups marinade. Cover and simmer 2 to 3 hours or until tender, basting and turning occasionally. When done, remove meat from Dutch oven and keep warm.

Strain sauce and skim off fat. Measure liquid to make two cups. Add about ¼ cup water to flour to make slurry. Mix into sauce. Stir until thick over medium heat. Add raisins and sour cream; mix well. To serve, slice meat and arrange on heated platter. Pour on a little sauce. Serve rest of sauce in separate bowl.

Kartoffelsalat
(Hot German Potato Salad)

SERVES 8

8	large boiling potatoes, diced ½ inch with skins on (about 8 cups cooked potatoes)
8	strips bacon
3	tablespoons bacon drippings
1	small onion, finely chopped (about ½ cup)
1	rib celery with leaves, finely chopped (about ½ cup)
2	dill pickles, finely chopped
⅓	cup water
¾	cup vinegar
2	teaspoons sugar
½	teaspoon salt
½	teaspoon paprika
½	teaspoon dry mustard

Chopped parsley and chives for garnish

Cook diced potatoes in covered saucepan until tender. Drain and set aside.

Cook bacon until crisp. Remove bacon; drain and crumble, reserving 3 tablespoons drippings.

Sauté onion and celery in drippings until translucent. Add chopped pickles. Set aside.

In separate saucepan, heat water and vinegar to boiling point. Add seasonings. Combine all ingredients, stirring until well mixed. Serve at once, garnished with chopped parsley and chives.

Rotkohl
(Braised Red Cabbage)

SERVES 8

2½	pounds red cabbage, shredded (about 8 cups)
6	tablespoons red wine vinegar
6	tablespoons water or stock (see p. 221)
⅓	cup sugar
1	large apple, peeled and chopped (about 1 cup)
2	teaspoons salt
1	teaspoon ground pepper
3	tablespoons butter (optional)
10	juniper berries, crushed (optional)

Combine all ingredients in large pot. Cover with buttered sheet of waxed paper and tight-fitting lid. Simmer over very low heat ½ hour; stir; add water if necessary. Taste to correct seasonings. Continue cooking additional ½ hour.

Serve hot or cold. Keeps in refrigerator for several weeks. Better if made day before serving and reheated. May also be cooked in 325° oven about 2 hours.

Chocolate Sauerkraut Cake

SERVES 16

2¼	cups cake flour
1	teaspoon baking powder
1	teaspoon baking soda
¼	teaspoon salt
½	cup Dutch cocoa
⅔	cup sauerkraut
⅔	cup butter
1½	cups sugar
3	large eggs
1	teaspoon vanilla extract (see p. 224)
1	cup water

Preheat oven to 350°.

Sift flour with baking powder, baking soda, salt, and cocoa. Set aside.

Rinse and drain sauerkraut. Snip into small pieces with kitchen scissors. Set aside.

Cream butter and sugar until light and fluffy. Add eggs, one at a time, beating well after each addition. Add vanilla extract. Stir in flour mixture, alternating with water. Fold in sauerkraut last.

Turn batter into 10-inch tube pan that has been buttered and sugared. Bake 35 to 40 minutes. Cool in pan 5 minutes. Remove from pan and cool on rack.

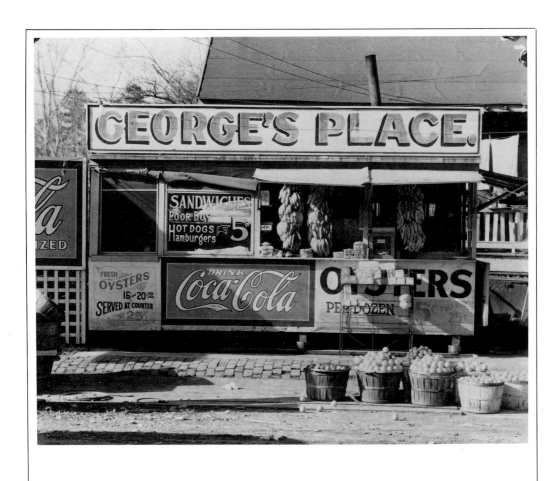

Roadside Sandwich Shop, Ponchatoula, Louisiana, *1936*
Photograph by Walker Evans
Target Collection of American Photography

for Six

⋆ Cold Day Soup

Assorted Greens with Vinaigrette (see p. 225)

⋆ French Bread Baguettes

⋆ Kiwi Crisp

Crisp fall days bring to mind warm soups and stews. These "jewels-of-the-one-dish-meal" are perfect for making ahead to transport to the farm, beach house, or hunting camp, ready to be served when reheated. A selection of alternate hearty dishes can be found in "Basics and Bonuses." Any one of those dishes could be substituted for the soup suggested here. A good Beaujolais is an excellent wine to accompany most of these dishes.

Cold Day Soup

YIELDS 2½ TO 3 QUARTS

1   2-pound package white beans (Great Northern preferred)
3   carrots, chopped (about 3 cups)
2   onions, chopped (about 1½ cups)
1½ cups finely chopped parsley
1   tablespoon sugar
2   tablespoons seasoned salt
½   teaspoon cracked pepper or to taste
2   rings smoked Polish sausage (about 3 pounds), casing removed, sliced ⅓ inch thick

Garnish:
Grated Monterey Jack cheese
Scallions, including green tops, finely chopped
Jalapeños, finely chopped

Wash beans; soak overnight.

Combine beans, carrots, onions, parsley, sugar, salt, and pepper. Cover with water; simmer about 1 hour or until beans are done but still firm. Add sausage; simmer until meat is done. Adjust seasonings.

Serve in hot soup bowls with side dishes of cheese, scallions, and jalapeños as desired. Soup is thick and may be thinned with additional water to produce desired consistency.

French Bread Baguettes

YIELDS 3 LOAVES

2½ cups warm water (110°)
2 packages active dry yeast
1 tablespoon salt
6 to 7 cups unbleached white flour
Melted butter
Cornmeal

Measure warm water in large mixing bowl. Add yeast, stirring with fork until dissolved. Stir in salt and 3 cups flour. Beat until batter is smooth. Gradually add enough flour to make a soft, workable dough.

Remove to floured board. Knead, adding more flour as necessary until smooth, elastic dough results. Place dough in large, warm buttered bowl. Turn to coat top with melted butter. Cover with plastic wrap and kitchen towel. Let dough triple in bulk (about 2½ hours).

Punch down; knead lightly in bowl. Cover and allow to double (about 1 hour).

Turn out on floured board. Divide into 3 portions. Cover; let rest 15 minutes.

Grease baguette pans; sprinkle with cornmeal. Roll each portion of dough into 9 × 16–inch rectangles. Roll into tight roll starting with long side. Pinch ends and edge to seal. Roll to desired length. Place on prepared baking pan, seam side down. Cover; let rise 1 hour.

Preheat oven to 450°.

Slash loaves with single-edged razor blade, diagonally, ½ inch deep. Use pastry brush to coat baguettes with cold water. Place loaves on middle shelf of oven. Using atomizer, quickly spray water to create steam. Set timer for 5 minutes. Spray again. Repeat 2 more times at 5-minute intervals. Bake additional 10 minutes. Total baking time is 25 minutes.

To reheat: Brush bread with cold water; warm in 400° oven about 10 minutes.

Kiwi Crisp

SERVES 6

½ cup flour
½ cup brown sugar
½ cup butter
¾ cup chopped pistachios, divided
½ cup sugar
⅛ teaspoon salt
⅓ cup potato starch
1 teaspoon grated lime zest
12 kiwi fruits, peeled and sliced (about 4 cups)

Work together flour, brown sugar, butter, and ½ cup pistachios to form topping. Set aside in refrigerator.

Preheat oven to 450°.

Mix together sugar, salt, potato starch, and lime zest. Mix gently with kiwis. Pour into 10-inch oven-proof dish. Cover with topping. Arrange remaining pistachios over top in attractive pattern. Bake 10 minutes. Reduce heat to 350°; bake additional 15 to 20 minutes or until topping is golden. Serve warm.

Corn shocks and rail fence near Marion, West Virginia, *1940*
Photograph by Marion Post Wolcott
Gift of Arthur Rothstein

HALLOWEEN TRICK-OR-TREAT SUPPER

for Eight

⋆ Pumpkin-Mushroom Bisque

⋆ Pastel de Choclo (Corn Pie)

⋆ Green Salad with Papaya Seed Dressing

French Bread (see p. 143)

⋆ Flan de Coco (Coconut Flan)

Pumpkin-Mushroom Bisque

SERVES 8 TO 10

8   tablespoons butter
1   pound mushrooms, sliced (about 2 cups)
1   large onion, chopped (about 1 cup)
⅓   cup flour
2   quarts strong chicken stock (see p. 221)
2   cups cooked fresh pumpkin
2   cups heavy cream
2   teaspoons honey
1 to 2 teaspoons curry powder or to taste
½   teaspoon salt or to taste
⅛   teaspoon ground white pepper or to taste

Garnish:
Sour cream
Chopped parsley
Sliced raw mushrooms
Buttered croutons
Freshly grated Parmesan cheese

Melt butter in large, heavy saucepan; sauté mushrooms over medium-high heat until golden brown. Remove. Add onion. Sauté until transparent. Add flour; mix well, cook 4 to 5 minutes. Do not brown. Add chicken stock and pumpkin. Bring to boil. Reduce heat; simmer about 20 minutes. Remove from heat.

Purée with mushrooms in processor or blender.

Return to pan; add cream, honey, and curry powder. Simmer additional 10 minutes. Salt and pepper to taste. Serve hot, garnished with all or selected garnishes.

Bisque is better if made day before serving. It could be served in hollowed-out pumpkin shell.

Pastel de Choclo
(Corn Pie)

SERVES 8

1   tablespoon vegetable oil
2   onions, finely chopped (about 1½ cups)
2   cloves garlic, finely chopped
1½   pounds lean ground beef
½   cup meat stock (see p. 220) or bouillon
½   cup seedless raisins
1   teaspoon cumin seed or ground cumin
2   teaspoons dried oregano
1½   teaspoons salt, divided
1¼   teaspoons ground black pepper, divided
20   ripe olives
2   hard-boiled eggs, chopped
5   ears fresh corn, cut off the cob, or 4 cups frozen whole kernel corn
1   tablespoon sugar
1   tablespoon flour
1   tablespoon chopped scallions
½   cup cream

In heavy skillet heat oil; sauté onions and garlic until translucent but not browned. Add beef, stock, raisins, cumin, oregano, ½ teaspoon salt, and ¼ teaspoon pepper. Simmer 30 minutes. Spoon mixture into three-quart casserole; scatter olives and chopped eggs over mixture.

Preheat oven to 375°.

In processor or blender, combine corn, sugar, flour, scallions, cream, and remaining salt and pepper. Process about 30 seconds. Pour over meat mixture. Bake 45 minutes. Allow to rest 5 to 10 minutes before serving.

Papaya Seed Dressing

YIELDS 3 CUPS

1   cup sugar
1   teaspoon dry mustard
1   teaspoon salt
1   cup tarragon or wine vinegar
2   cups vegetable oil
1   small onion, finely chopped (about ½ cup)
3   tablespoons fresh papaya seeds

Place all dry ingredients and vinegar in blender. Turn blender on and gradually add oil and onion. When thoroughly blended, add papaya seeds. Blend only until seeds are size of coarse ground pepper. Use on fruit or tossed green salad.

Flan de Coco
(Coconut Flan)

SERVES 8

4   eggs
1   13-ounce can evaporated milk
1   14-ounce can sweetened condensed milk
¼   teaspoon ground cinnamon
¼   teaspoon grated nutmeg
1   teaspoon vanilla extract (see p. 224)
1   cup sugar
1   cup grated coconut, fresh or frozen

Preheat oven to 350°.
Beat eggs; add rest of ingredients except sugar and coconut. Set aside.
In 9-inch metal pie pan melt sugar and allow to brown to make caramel. Put pie pan in pan of water. Pour in milk mixture; sprinkle coconut on top. Bake 1 hour or until knife inserted in center comes out clean.

Note: If only canned coconut is available, put in colander. Rinse thoroughly with cold water to remove sugar. Drain well.

Hunting Still Life, *1890*
Painting by Richard Goodwin
Gift of the Junior League of Houston

for Six

*Avocado Halves with Piquante Sauce

*Dove Casserole

Wild Rice

Green Salad

*Lemon Velvet Ice Cream

*Oatmeal Butterscotch Cookies

Barolo or Chianti Classico

Texas is on the central flyway for migratory birds that move from Canada to Mexico and South America each fall and back again to nest in Canada in the spring. White-winged doves migrate in the early fall, followed in a few weeks by ducks and geese. Many of these birds spend an entire winter in rice fields or marshes along the shoreline where there are grain and fish to eat and trees and grasses in which to roost and hide. Some of the best bird shooting in the United States is to be found along this avian highway.

A very popular nonmigratory bird, the quail, is found in a large portion of the state, particularly in South Texas. Both quails and pheasants—which are now beginning to naturalize in parts of the state—provide exciting sport as well as delicious dishes.

Preparing game birds is as challenging and interesting as bagging them. Dove, duck, and quail are featured in this and the following two menus.

Avocado Halves with Piquante Sauce

YIELDS SAUCE FOR 6 AVOCADO HALVES

3   tablespoons Worcestershire sauce
3   tablespoons vinegar
2   tablespoons butter
3   tablespoons catsup or chili sauce
⅛   teaspoon sugar
Salt and pepper to taste

Heat ingredients in saucepan. Serve hot in chilled avocado halves.

Dove Casserole

SERVES 6

1   small onion, chopped (about ½ cup)
1   small rib celery, chopped (about ½ cup)
½   pound butter
2   tablespoons Worcestershire sauce
2   teaspoons dry sherry
1   teaspoon salt
1   teaspoon freshly ground white pepper
¼   pound fresh mushrooms, sliced
12 to 16 doves, cleaned

Preheat oven to 275°.
Sauté onion and celery in butter until translucent but not browned. Add Worcestershire sauce, sherry, salt, and pepper. Add mushrooms.
Arrange doves in oven-proof casserole; cover with vegetables. Cover; bake 2 hours or until tender. Baste several times during cooking. If necessary to brown, uncover at end of cooking time. Skim off fat. Serve over wild rice with pan juices.

Lemon Velvet Ice Cream

YIELDS ½ GALLON

Juice of 3 oranges
Juice of 4½ lemons
Grated zest of 3 lemons
3¾ cups sugar
⅜ teaspoon salt
1 pint heavy cream
1½ quarts milk

Mix together juices, zest, and sugar. Add salt, cream, and milk. Freeze in electric freezer per manufacturer's directions.

Oatmeal Butterscotch Cookies

YIELDS 5 DOZEN

12 tablespoons butter
¾ cup light brown sugar, firmly packed
¼ cup sugar
1 large egg, beaten lightly
1 teaspoon vanilla extract (see p. 224)
¾ cup flour
⅛ teaspoon salt
½ teaspoon baking soda
1⅔ cups old-fashioned rolled oats
6 ounces butterscotch chips
¼ cup chopped pecans

Cream butter and sugars. Add egg and vanilla extract. Beat until light and fluffy.

Sift flour, salt, and baking soda. Blend into sugar mixture; add oats, butterscotch chips, and pecans. Chill dough 30 minutes.

Form into 2 large 1- to 1½-inch diameter rolls. Roll tightly in wax paper. Refrigerate several hours or overnight.

Preheat oven to 375°.

Cut dough into ¼-inch slices. Place on greased baking sheet and bake 8 to 10 minutes.

Wild Turkey, *ca. 1827–1838*
Engraving after John James Audubon
Bayou Bend Collection, Gift of Miss Ima Hogg

QUAIL DINNER

for Six

∗ Melon Appetizer

∗ Quail Bavarian

∗ Baked Rice with Mushrooms

∗ Fresh Spinach

∗ Refrigerator Rolls

∗ Lemon Curd Tarts

Mersault

Melon Appetizer

SERVES 6

2   medium-size cantaloupes or 1 large honeydew melon
1   cup port wine
1   teaspoon powdered ginger or 2 teaspoons finely chopped preserved ginger
¼   pound prosciutto, very thinly sliced
Cracked black pepper (optional)
Lime wedges (optional)

Peel and seed melons. Cut into slices; arrange in flat, nonmetallic pan. Add port wine and ginger. Cover; refrigerate several hours.

Divide melon among 6 plates. Roll or twist slices of prosciutto around slices of melon or intersperse with melon. Spoon marinade over each portion. Serve with cracked black pepper and lime wedges if desired.

Quail Bavarian

SERVES 6

12   whole quail, cleaned
8   tablespoons butter
2   large green apples, peeled, cored, and coarsely chopped (about 2 cups)
½   cup brandy
2   teaspoons salt
½   teaspoon ground white pepper
¼   cup fresh lemon juice
2   cups heavy cream
1   tablespoon cornstarch
1   tablespoon cold water

Preheat oven to 375°.

Melt butter in heavy skillet. Sauté quail until browned. Remove. Add apples to skillet; sauté until lightly browned. Remove. Place apples in large casserole. Put quail on top of apples.

Meanwhile, deglaze skillet with brandy; pour over birds. Cover and bake 30 minutes.

Remove from oven; sprinkle with salt and pepper. Add lemon juice; cover with cream. Bake uncovered additional 15 minutes. Remove birds to serving platter.

Mix cornstarch with water; add to pan drippings, stirring until thickened. Pour sauce over birds before serving.

Baked Rice with Mushrooms

SERVES 6

8   tablespoons butter
1   cup uncooked rice
1   onion, finely chopped (about ¾ cup)
2½ cups beef broth (see p. 220) or 1
     10-ounce can plus 1 can water
8   ounces fresh mushrooms, sliced, or 1
     4-ounce can sliced mushrooms with
     liquid
1   teaspoon salt
1   teaspoon dried oregano

Preheat oven to 275°.

Melt butter in skillet; add rice and onion. Sauté about 5 minutes, stirring constantly. Add broth, mushrooms with liquid, salt, and oregano. Pour into 2-quart casserole; bake, uncovered, 1½ hours. Stir occasionally.

Fresh Spinach

SERVES 6

2   10-ounce packages fresh spinach
6   slices bacon
¾   teaspoon salt
½   teaspoon freshly ground black pepper
¼   teaspoon garlic salt or ½ clove garlic,
     pressed
2   hard-boiled eggs, shelled and finely
     chopped

Wash spinach thoroughly. Remove tough stems; shake dry.

Fry bacon until crisp; set aside. Remove all fat except 2 tablespoons. Add spinach, salt, pepper, and garlic salt or fresh garlic. Cook over low heat just long enough to wilt spinach. Remove to serving dish. Top with crumbled bacon and hard-boiled eggs.

Refrigerator Rolls

YIELDS 2 DOZEN

2   packages active dry yeast
¼   cup warm water (110°)
1½ cups milk
6   tablespoons sugar
½   cup shortening
1   teaspoon salt
4½ cups flour
2   large eggs
Melted butter

Dissolve yeast in warm water. Set aside.

Combine milk, sugar, shortening, and salt. Heat in saucepan until shortening is melted and sugar and salt are dissolved. Cool to 110°.

Combine yeast and milk mixtures with flour and eggs in processor; process until well combined. Or mix together in large bowl with wooden spoon.

Turn dough out on lightly floured board; knead until smooth and elastic. Place in greased bowl; turn to coat well. Cover and let rise until doubled in bulk. Punch down and use at once or completely wrap in plastic and refrigerate. Keeps well 4 to 7 days.

When ready to bake: preheat oven to 425°.

Pinch off amount desired. Roll out dough. Cut in desired shape. Place in greased pans just touching or on greased cookie sheets 2 inches apart. Allow to rise until doubled in size (about 30 minutes for freshly made dough or 3 to 4 hours for refrigerated dough). Brush with cooled melted butter; bake 10 to 15 minutes.

Variation: Follow above recipe substituting 1½ cups buttermilk for whole milk. Add ½ teaspoon baking soda to flour and omit eggs. Buttermilk rolls are better if baked immediately after making.

Lemon Curd Tarts

YIELDS 10 TARTS

8   tablespoons butter
2   lemons, juice and zest
1   cup sugar
4   eggs
⅛   teaspoon salt
10 2-inch baked pastry shells (see p. 254)
½   cup whipped cream for garnish

Melt butter. Remove zest with peeler. Add to sugar in processor or blender. Process until zest is finely chopped. Add juice, sugar, and zest to butter. Mix thoroughly. Beat eggs well; add to mixture. Add salt.

Place mixture in top of double boiler over hot water; cook until thickened, stirring constantly. Remove from heat; cool. Fill pastry shells with mixture; garnish with whipped cream, if desired.

DUCK DINNER

for Four

∗Oyster-Artichoke Soup

∗Ragout of Duck

Steamed Rice

Sautéed Green Beans with Lemon-Butter Sauce

∗Cranberry Upside-Down Cake with Orange Custard Sauce

Montrachet

Pheasant Dish, ca. 1756–1769
Chelsea Porcelain Works
Gift of Mr. and Mrs. Harris Masterson

Oyster-Artichoke Soup

SERVES 4

4 tablespoons butter
1 clove garlic, finely chopped
½ medium onion, chopped (about ¼ cup)
⅛ cup flour
1½ 8½-ounce cans artichoke hearts, quartered and drained
1 quart double chicken stock (see p. 221)
¼ teaspoon red pepper
¼ teaspoon anise seed
½ teaspoon salt
1½ teaspoons Worcestershire sauce
1 pint or 2 10-ounce jars oysters, drained and blended 30 seconds

Melt butter in large saucepan. Sauté garlic and onion until translucent but not browned. Add flour, artichoke hearts, stock, and seasonings; simmer 15 minutes. Add oysters; simmer until heated (about 10 minutes). Do not boil. May be kept in refrigerator 2 to 3 days. Freezes well.

Note: Canned broth or instant granules can be substituted for double stock, but soup will not be as rich or smooth.

Ragout of Duck

SERVES 4

8 tablespoons butter
2 tablespoons flour
4 tablespoons finely chopped cooked ham
6 tablespoons finely chopped onion
6 tablespoons finely chopped celery
4 tablespoons finely chopped mild red or green bell pepper
4 tablespoons finely chopped parsley
2 cups veal stock (see p. 220 and 221)
½ cup dry red wine
½ cup beer
1 teaspoon salt
1 teaspoon ground pepper
1 teaspoon paprika
1 clove
¼ teaspoon ground coriander
⅛ teaspoon ground mace or less
⅛ teaspoon grated nutmeg or less
2 to 4 tablespoons jalapeño jelly
2 cups cubed cooked duck pieces

Melt butter in large saucepan; stir in flour. Cook 1 to 2 minutes. Stir in ham, onion, celery, pepper, and parsley. Add stock, wine, beer, and seasonings; mix well. Reduce heat. Cover; simmer 45 minutes. Add jalapeño jelly to taste. Continue to cook 15 minutes.

Strain mixture; stir in duck. Cook just long enough to heat meat thoroughly. Serve over rice.

Cranberry Upside-Down Cake
with Orange Custard Sauce

SERVES 6 TO 8

9   tablespoons butter, divided
1   cup sugar, divided
1   pound fresh cranberries
1   egg
1   teaspoon vanilla extract (see p. 224)
1   teaspoon grated orange zest
1¼ cups flour
¼   teaspoon salt
1¼ teaspoons baking powder
½   cup milk
⅓   cup currant jelly, melted

Orange Custard Sauce
1   cup milk
1   cup half-and-half
1   1-inch piece vanilla bean
3   pieces orange zest (3½ × ½ inch each)
6   egg yolks
¼   cup sugar
2   tablespoons Grand Marnier

Preheat oven to 350°.

Spread bottom and sides of 9-inch cake pan with 3 tablespoons butter. Sprinkle ½ cup sugar on bottom of pan evenly; cover with cranberries.

Cream remaining butter and sugar. Add egg, vanilla extract, and orange zest; mix well. Sift together flour, salt, and baking powder. Add flour mixture to butter-sugar mixture alternately with milk. Mix just until combined.

Pour mixture over cranberries. Smooth top; bake about 1 hour or until well browned. Cool on rack 20 minutes. Invert on plate. Brush with melted currant jelly.

To make sauce: In saucepan, bring to simmer milk, half-and-half, vanilla bean, and orange zest. Remove from heat; let stand 15 minutes.

Beat egg yolks; add sugar. Strain milk mixture; add to egg mixture. Add liqueur. Cook, stirring constantly, until mixture thickens slightly and coats back of wooden spoon. Cool before pouring. Serve separately in sauceboat to pour over cake.

English Needlepoint Slip Seat, ca. 1730
Bayou Bend Collection, Gift of Miss Ima Hogg

SUNDAY LUNCH

for Six

⋆ Spiced Pork Tenderloin

⋆ Snow Peas in Seasoned Butter

⋆ Peanut Rice

⋆ Baked Pears in Cream

Chardonnay

Spiced Pork Tenderloin

SERVES 6

1 cup chicken broth (see p. 221)
¼ cup soy sauce
¼ cup vegetable oil
¼ cup honey
2 tablespoons sherry
1 tablespoon lemon juice
½ teaspoon ground cinnamon
1 clove garlic, pressed
1 teaspoon salt
3 pork tenderloins (¾ pound each)
2 tablespoons cornstarch

Sauce:
¾ cup unsalted chicken stock or ½ cup dry white wine plus ¼ cup water
3 tablespoons butter

Combine broth, soy sauce, vegetable oil, honey, sherry, lemon juice, cinnamon, garlic, and salt. Marinate pork in mixture for several hours or overnight in refrigerator.

Preheat oven to 325°.

Drain meat; roll in cornstarch. Bake 1½ hours, basting frequently with marinade. Remove from pan, cover, and keep warm.

To make sauce: Add stock to defatted pan drippings, scraping to incorporate all browned bits. Reduce to ½ cup. Swirl in butter, taste to correct seasonings.

Slice meat on diagonal and arrange on serving platter. Spoon sauce over slices.

Snow Peas in Seasoned Butter

SERVES 6

1 pound snow peas
1 quart boiling water
1 tablespoon salt
2 tablespoons butter
1 shallot, finely chopped
1 clove garlic, pressed
Salt to taste

Remove strings from peas. Cook in boiling salted water 1 minute. Drain; run under cold water.

Melt butter in skillet; add shallots and garlic. Sauté until translucent. Add snow peas; sauté 1 minute to coat with butter. Remove from heat. Salt to taste.

Peanut Rice

SERVES 6

4	cups hot cooked white rice (about 1¼ cups uncooked)
½	cup chopped roasted peanuts
4	tablespoons butter, melted
¼	cup honey
¼	teaspoon ground cinnamon
1	teaspoon powdered sugar

Watercress for garnish

Combine all ingredients except watercress in 1½-quart casserole. Cover; keep warm until serving time. Top with sprig of watercress.

Baked Pears in Cream

SERVES 6

6	pears, ripe but firm
⅓	cup sugar
2	tablespoons butter, cut into small pieces
¾	cup orange-flavored liqueur (Grand Marnier or Triple Sec), divided
1	cup whipping cream
⅓	cup finely chopped toasted almonds

Preheat oven to 400°.

Peel, core, and halve pears. Place cut side down in single layer in 9 × 13–inch baking dish. Sprinkle pears with sugar; dot with butter. Add ½ cup liqueur. Bake 35 to 40 minutes or until tender.

Remove from oven. Reduce heat to 350°. Pour cream over pears; return to oven. Baste several times while cooking 15 minutes or until cream is thickened and caramel color. Cool at room temperature. Before serving, sprinkle remaining liqueur and chopped almonds over pears. Serve at room temperature.

New England Rooster Weathervane, ca. 1850–1875
Iron, Artist unknown
Bayou Bend Collection, Gift of Miss Ima Hogg

for Eight

⋆ Cold Jellied Borsch

⋆ Cornish Game Hens

Brown Rice

⋆ Carrots in Cointreau Sauce

⋆ Upside-Down Apple Tart

Pinot Grigio

Cold Jellied Borsch

SERVES 8

1   16-ounce can cut beets
1   small onion, chopped (about ⅓ cup)
1   small wedge cabbage, chopped (about
     ½ cup)
1   10½-ounce can consommé
½   cup tomato juice
1   teaspoon salt
Pepper to taste
2   tablespoons cider vinegar
1   tablespoon unflavored gelatin
3   tablespoons cold water
½   pint sour cream for garnish
½   teaspoon horseradish or to taste

Blend beets with liquid, onion, and cabbage in processor or blender until puréed. Pour into saucepan; add consommé, tomato juice, salt, pepper, and vinegar. Simmer 15 minutes.

Soften gelatin in water; stir into hot beet mixture until fully dissolved. Chill until thickened (4 to 6 hours). Serve with sour cream seasoned with horseradish.

Cornish Game Hens

SERVES 8

8   Cornish game hens (20 ounces each)
1   teaspoon salt or to taste
1   teaspoon ground white pepper
½   teaspoon ground allspice
2   tablespoons crushed garlic
2   teaspoons dried thyme
¾   pound butter, divided
2   pounds fresh mushrooms, thinly sliced,
     divided
2   cups dry white wine
2   tablespoons dried Italian seasoning

Preheat oven to 350°.

Clean birds; drain and dry. Mix salt, pepper, allspice, garlic, and thyme; rub birds inside and out. Set aside.

Melt 8 tablespoons butter; sauté ½ pound mushrooms until golden brown. Put into cavities of birds.

Melt remaining butter. Add remaining mushrooms, wine, and Italian seasoning. Pour over birds.

With breast down, bake 45 minutes to 1 hour, basting every 15 minutes. Turn oven to 400°. Turn hens; with breast side up, bake 10 minutes or until brown.

Carrots in Cointreau Sauce

SERVES 8

1½ pounds carrots
4   tablespoons butter
2   tablespoons brown sugar
1   teaspoon grated orange zest
¼   cup Cointreau
Chopped parsley for garnish

Peel carrots; cut into julienne strips about 3 × ¼ inch. Cook until barely tender in salted water (about 10 minutes). Drain; refresh briefly under cold water. Set aside.

In heavy skillet melt butter; add brown sugar. Stir over low heat until sugar melts. Add orange zest; cook 1 to 2 minutes to extract oil. Add Cointreau; mix well. Add carrots; toss gently until coated with glaze. Heat. Sprinkle parsley over carrots. Serve immediately.

Upside-Down Apple Tart

SERVES 6 TO 8

Apple Filling:
½   cup butter
6   large apples (Newton, Pippin, Granny Smith, Winesap), peeled, cored, and thinly sliced
½   cup sugar
1   teaspoon grated lemon zest

Caramel:
½   cup sugar
3   tablespoons water
¼   teaspoon cream of tartar

Pâté brisée for 9-inch crust (see p. 254)

Preheat oven to 475°.
In large skillet melt butter. Add apples, sugar, and lemon zest. Carefully toss apples to coat. Cook until soft. Transfer to baking sheet and cool.

In small heavy saucepan cook sugar, water, and cream of tartar until honey color. Pour into hot 9-inch pie tin, tilting pan to spread evenly. Arrange apples over set caramel and cover with pastry. Do not trim. Allow about ½-inch edge of pastry to fall over rim of pie tin.

Heat baking sheet in center of oven. Place tart on baking sheet. Lower heat to 375°; bake 50 minutes or until crust is brown. Cool on rack at least 30 minutes before carefully inverting on serving plate.

Untitled from Oaxaca Series, *1980*
Photograph by Serge Hambourg
Gift of Mr. and Mrs. Benjamin Kitchen III

168

SOUTH OF THE BORDER DINNER

for Six

＊Chili con Queso (Chile with Cheese)

Tostados and Salsa

＊Guacamole Dip (Avocado Dip)

＊Carne Guisada with Game (Meat Stew with Game)

＊Pico de Gallo (Vegetable Relish)

＊Frijoles Refritos (Refried Beans)

Sliced Mangos with Lime Juice

Beer

Coffee

Chili con Queso
(Chile with Cheese)

SERVES 6

1   pound processed American cheese
1   tablespoon vegetable oil
2   cloves garlic, pressed
1   white onion, chopped (about ½ to ⅔ cup)
1   10-ounce can tomatoes and chilies
½   teaspoon ground cumin
Fried tortilla chips

Cut processed cheese into small chunks; place in double boiler. Heat until melted.

Heat oil in skillet; sauté garlic and onion until translucent. Combine garlic-onion mixture, tomatoes, and cumin. Add melted cheese. Stir until tomatoes are broken and mixture is smooth. Keep hot. Serve with fried tortilla chips.

Guacamole Dip
(Avocado Dip)

SERVES 6

2   medium tomatoes, peeled and finely chopped
6   scallions, finely chopped
1   tablespoon finely chopped cilantro
4   medium avocados
Juice of 3 limes
¼   teaspoon salt
Pepper to taste
Toasted tortilla chips

Mix tomatoes, scallions, and cilantro.

Peel and mash avocados. Add lime juice, salt, and pepper. Mix avocados and tomatoes. Do not overmix or it will lose color and texture. Serve with toasted tortilla chips.

Carne Guisada with Game
(Meat Stew with Game)

SERVES 6

2   pounds venison, elk, or beef cut into
    2 × ½–inch strips (use backstrap or
    round steak)
1½ teaspoons salt
1   teaspoon ground black pepper
¼   teaspoon Cayenne pepper or ½ teaspoon
    chili powder
1   teaspoon dried oregano
1   teaspoon ground cumin
2 or 3 tablespoons vegetable oil
1   medium white onion, finely chopped
    (about ½ cup)
3   chilies poblano* or 1 large green bell
    pepper, seeded and cut into strips (about
    1 cup)
3   cloves garlic, pressed
1   10-ounce can tomatoes and green chilies
½   cup fresh lime juice

Place meat in bowl. Mix together salt
and spices; sprinkle over meat, tossing to
coat completely.

Heat oil in skillet. Brown meat. Add
onion, poblano or green pepper strips,
and garlic. Sauté vegetables slightly. Add
tomatoes and green chilies; simmer 30
minutes or until meat is tender. Add lime
juice; cook 10 to 15 minutes.

* See tips on peeling peppers (p. 217).

Pico de Gallo
(Vegetable Relish)

SERVES 6

2   large tomatoes, peeled and finely
    chopped
1   large white onion, finely chopped (about
    ¾ cup)
1   large clove garlic, pressed
1 to 2 tablespoons finely chopped cilantro
1 to 2 jalapeño chilies, seeded and finely
    chopped
1   head iceberg lettuce, shredded
Salt and pepper to taste

Combine all ingredients; mix well.

Frijoles Refritos
(Refried Beans)

SERVES 6

8   ounces dried small red pinto beans
5 to 6 cups water
1   large onion, finely chopped (about 1
    cup), divided
2   cloves garlic, pressed
1   tablespoon bacon drippings
1½ tablespoons salt
8   tablespoons lard or bacon drippings

Combine beans, water, ½ cup onion,
garlic, and bacon drippings in large saucepan; bring to boil. Reduce heat, cover, and
simmer 1½ to 2 hours. Add salt; cook additional 15 minutes.

In large heavy skillet, heat lard or bacon
drippings. Add remaining onion; cook until soft. Add enough beans to cover bottom
of skillet. Turn heat to high. With potato
masher, mash beans; add some liquid from
beans. Continue this process until all beans
are mashed and mixture becomes paste.
Cook additional 15 to 20 minutes until
beans are semidry and edges are crispy.
Serve immediately.

Cyclamen in Restaurant Garden

Winter Menus

WINTER SUNDAY NIGHT SUPPER

for Eight

⁕ Pinto Bean Soup in the Magyar Manner

Open-Face Rye Bread and Cheese Toasted Sandwiches

⁕ Coffee Spice Cake

Zinfandel

Silver Tankard, ca. 1695–1711
By John Coney
Bayou Bend Collection, Gift of Miss Ima Hogg

Pinto Bean Soup in the Magyar Manner

YIELDS 3½ QUARTS

2½ cups pinto beans
8 cups water
Meaty ham bone or 2 ham hocks
¼ teaspoon freshly ground pepper or to taste
3 bay leaves
2 ribs celery, chopped (about 1 cup)
2 carrots, chopped (about 1 cup)
1 medium turnip, chopped (about ½ cup)
½ pound smoked fully cooked sausage (such as Kielbasa), casing removed, cut into ¼-inch rounds
4 tablespoons butter
2 tablespoons flour
½ cup finely chopped onion
1 large clove garlic, finely chopped
½ cup finely chopped parsley
2 tablespoons Worcestershire sauce
2 teaspoons Hungarian hot paprika or to taste
Sour cream for garnish

Wash beans and pick over thoroughly. Cover with water, about 3 inches. Soak overnight.

Drain, reserving liquid. Measure liquid; increase to 8 cups. Combine with beans in stock pot. Add ham bone or hocks, pepper, and bay leaves. Simmer 1 hour.

Add celery, carrots, and turnips. Simmer 45 minutes. Remove ham bone or hocks from pot. Cut meat from bones and cube. Return to pot. Add sausage.

In small saucepan, melt butter. Add flour; blend well. Add onion, garlic, parsley, Worcestershire sauce, and paprika. Mix well; cook about 3 minutes. Add to beans, stirring well. Simmer 15 minutes. Correct seasonings. Serve hot, garnished with sour cream.

Note: When reheating, add more water and paprika if necessary.

Coffee Spice Cake

SERVES 8

2 cups brown sugar
2 cups flour, sifted
½ cup butter
½ teaspoon salt
2 tablespoons instant coffee
1 teaspoon ground cinnamon
½ cup chopped nuts
½ teaspoon grated nutmeg
1 teaspoon baking soda
1 cup sour cream
1 egg

Topping:
1 cup whipping cream
1 teaspoon sugar
1 teaspoon grated orange zest
1 to 2 tablespoons orange liqueur

Preheat oven to 350°.

Mix sugar, flour, butter, salt, coffee, cinnamon, and nuts until texture is like coarse crumbs. Place half of mixture in buttered 9-inch square pan.

Mix nutmeg, baking soda, sour cream, and egg; combine with remaining half of crumb mixture. Mix well. Spoon over first layer.

Bake 40 to 50 minutes or until done. Cut into squares.

To make topping: Whip cream and fold in flavorings. Serve on freshly baked warm cake.

Madonna and Child, *before 1405*
Master of the Straus Madonna
Edith A. and Percy S. Straus Collection

A SPECIAL CHRISTMAS FEAST

for Eight

* Mulled Claret

* Pepper Wafers

* Roast Goose with Apricot Stuffing

* Baked Carrot Ring with Purée of Brussels Sprouts

* Winter Apple Salad

* Date-Nut Cake with Creamy Bourbon Sauce

Fruity Red or White Burgundy or Côte de Rhone

Mulled Claret

SERVES 8

1 cup water
¼ cup sugar
12 cloves
3-inch stick cinnamon
Peel of ½ lemon and ½ orange
1 bottle claret
8 lemon slices

In saucepan, combine water, sugar, spices, and fruit peels. Bring to boil; reduce heat and simmer 10 minutes. Strain mixture into another, larger saucepan; add wine and simmer 5 minutes longer. Pour mulled wine into 8 goblets and garnish each with lemon slice.

Pepper Wafers

YIELDS 8 TO 10 DOZEN

⅓ cup shortening
½ cup butter
⅓ cup boiling water
2 cups flour
½ teaspoon baking powder
1 teaspoon salt
⅓ pound grated cheese (½ Romano, ½ mozzarella)
2 tablespoons green peppercorns, freeze dried or water packed, well drained

Combine shortening and butter in mixing bowl. Pour in hot water and whip until well creamed. Set aside.

Sift flour, baking powder, and salt together. Mix into creamed shortening. Stir in grated cheese and form into flat ball. Wrap in plastic wrap and chill several hours.

Preheat oven to 350°.

When ready to use, roll out on lightly floured surface. Sprinkle with green peppercorns and fold pastry over to enclose them. Roll out again to about ¼-inch thickness. Cut into small rounds (about ¾ inch) or into sticks ¼ × 4 inches. Place on ungreased baking sheet; bake approximately 15 minutes or until crisp and golden brown.

Roast Goose with Apricot Stuffing

SERVES 8

1   goose (9-pounds) or 2 wild geese (3½ pounds each)

Stuffing:
1   30-ounce can apricot halves packed in light syrup
¼   cup butter
Liver from goose, if using domestic bird
1   onion, finely chopped (about 1 cup)
¼   cup finely chopped celery
¼   cup finely chopped green bell pepper (optional)
1   teaspoon salt
¼   teaspoon ground white pepper
¼   teaspoon ground nutmeg
4   cups cooked brown rice (about 1⅓ cups raw)
½   cup raisins
½   cup wheat germ
⅔   cup slivered toasted almonds

Sauce:
1½ cups defatted pan juices from goose or chicken stock (see p. 221)
4   teaspoons cornstarch
1   cup reserved apricot syrup
¼   cup apricot brandy
Watercress for garnish

Preheat oven to 425°.
Wash goose. Pat dry and salt lightly. Set aside until ready to stuff. Do not stuff until ready to cook.

To make stuffing: Drain apricots, reserving liquid. Set aside 8 apricot halves for garnish; chop remaining halves into quarters.
Melt butter in large heavy skillet. Add liver and sauté until pink. Remove from pan and chop; set aside. Add onion, celery, and optional green pepper; sauté until golden. Remove pan from heat; stir in rest of ingredients, chopped apricots, and liver. Mix well, scraping bottom of pan to remove any browned bits. Stuff goose; place on rack in roasting pan. If using domestic bird, prick skin over entire body, except drumsticks.

Brown goose 15 minutes in hot oven; reduce heat to 350° and continue roasting. Baste every 15 minutes with a little hot water to remove accumulated fat. Roast 2 to 2½ hours until drumsticks move easily and juices run pale yellow. Do not overcook.
If using wild goose, rub with butter and place in 350° oven. Cover loosely with foil and roast about 2 hours, basting every 15 minutes with drippings. There will not be as much drippings as for domestic goose. Test for doneness; do not overcook. Remove goose from oven; cover loosely with foil and keep warm while making sauce.

To make sauce: Pour off fat from pan. Measure defatted juices and adjust to make 1½ cups with chicken stock; reduce if there is a larger amount.
Dissolve cornstarch in a little water and add to reserved apricot syrup. Pour into pan with stock; bring to boil, stirring to remove browned bits. Reduce heat and cook until sauce is clear and thick (7 to 10 minutes).
Strain into saucepan; add apricot brandy and reserved halves. Heat apricots, remove and use to garnish platter. Spoon some sauce over bird; garnish with watercress. Serve sauce separately in heated sauceboat.

Baked Carrot Ring
with Purée of Brussels Sprouts

SERVES 8

12 tablespoons vegetable shortening
½ cup dark brown sugar
1 egg, slightly beaten
1 tablespoon water
1¼ cups flour
½ teaspoon baking soda
1 teaspoon baking powder
½ teaspoon salt
½ teaspoon ground cinnamon (scant)
½ teaspoon grated nutmeg
2½ cups grated raw carrots (about 1 pound)

Purée of Brussels Sprouts:
2 10-ounce packages frozen Brussels sprouts
1 teaspoon salt
¼ cup water
½ small clove garlic
⅓ cup olive oil
⅛ teaspoon sugar

Cream together shortening and brown sugar until fluffy. Add egg and water; mix well. Sift together flour, baking soda, baking powder, salt, and spices; add to sugar mixture. Fold in carrots. Cover and refrigerate 1 hour or longer.

Preheat oven to 350°.

Grease 9-inch ring mold; spoon batter into it. Place on center shelf of oven and bake about 50 minutes or until firm to the touch. Turn out on heated serving platter and slice at table. Center may be filled with tiny green peas, barely cooked and seasoned with butter and small amount of chopped scallions, or vegetable purée.

To make puree: In heavy saucepan, place sprouts, salt, and water. Cover and bring just to boil over high heat. Reduce heat immediately to low; cook about 15 minutes until sprouts are very tender.

Remove from heat. Drain. Add garlic, olive oil, and sugar. Purée until smooth. Return to heat and stir until piping hot. For milder garlic taste, add garlic to sprouts at beginning and cook together.

Winter Apple Salad

SERVES 8

2 bunches watercress
2 heads Belgian endive, thinly sliced
1 clove garlic
½ teaspoon rock salt
4 tablespoons white wine vinegar
¼ cup olive oil
¼ cup vegetable oil
½ teaspoon sugar
¼ teaspoon dry mustard
Cracked pepper
2 red Delicious apples, peeled and thinly sliced
½ cup dry bread crumbs, browned in butter
1 tablespoon coarsely ground walnuts
Cinnamon to sprinkle

Wash and dry watercress and endive. In wooden salad bowl rubbed with garlic, dissolve rock salt in wine vinegar. Add oils, sugar, mustard, and pepper. Add apples and salad greens; toss. Sprinkle with bread crumbs, walnuts, and cinnamon.

Date-Nut Cake
with Creamy Bourbon Sauce

SERVES 12

1   16-ounce package chopped dates
1½ teaspoons baking soda
1   cup boiling water
1½ cups dark brown sugar
2   tablespoons shortening
2   eggs
1½ cups chopped pecans
1½ teaspoons vanilla extract (see p. 224)
2¼ cups whole wheat flour
¼   teaspoon salt
¼   cup bourbon (optional)

Bourbon Sauce:
1   cup sugar
¼   pound butter
1   egg, beaten
4   tablespoons water
1   cup whipping cream
¼   cup bourbon or to taste

Preheat oven to 325°.

Sprinkle baking soda over dates. Pour boiling water over mixture. Set aside.

Cream sugar and shortening. Add eggs to creamed mixture and beat. Add nuts and vanilla extract. Stir until blended. Add date mixture and mix well. Add flour and salt and mix well.

Bake in greased and floured 9½-inch tube pan 45 to 50 minutes or until fork comes out clean when inserted.

Cool in pan. Remove from pan; cool. Pour bourbon over cake. Wrap in foil and store in refrigerator at least 2 weeks (up to 1 month) before serving.

To make sauce: Cream sugar and butter well. Add egg; beat until mixture is light and creamy. Put mixture in heavy saucepan with water. Cook over low heat, stirring constantly until thick. Remove from heat; cool.

Whip cream; fold into sauce. Add bourbon to taste.

Variation: Brandy, wine, or ¼ teaspoon ground allspice can be substituted for bourbon.

Still Life, 1656
Oil painting by Willem Claasz Heda
Gift of Mr. and Mrs. Raymond H. Goodrich

for Eight

Dry Champagne

* Brie en Croûte (Brie in Pastry)

* Chilled Broccoli with Sauce Piquante

* Duck Breasts Calvados

* Oven-Baked Herb Rice

* Kahlua-Mocha Mousse

Sharing a festive dinner with a few close friends is a special way to spend New Year's Eve. Champagne with Brie en croûte served before a crackling fire, followed by a dinner that features the most delectable duck breasts imaginable, is a grand finale to a good year as well as being the perfect greeting to the next. A California Cabernet Sauvignon, Private Reserve, is a natural wine choice to enhance the rich flavor of duck. Or, if you choose to substitute chicken breasts, try a big Chardonnay. Happy New Year!

Brie en Croûte
(Brie in Pastry)

YIELDS 4 TO 6 SMALL PORTIONS *

2   ounces cream cheese
4   tablespoons butter, chilled
½   cup flour
4   teaspoons cold water
1   4½-ounce package Brie or Camembert cheese
1   egg yolk

Make pastry one day ahead of serving time. Cut cream cheese and butter into flour until mixture resembles coarse meal. Add cold water; mix until dough forms ball. Wrap in plastic; refrigerate overnight.

Three hours before serving, roll out 8-inch circle of pastry; place Brie in center and encase. Cut hole in center of pastry for steam. Refrigerate.

One hour before serving apply egg wash. Return to refrigerator.

Thirty minutes before serving preheat oven to 450°. Bake 20 minutes or until pastry is lightly browned.

*Double recipe to make 2 pastries for this dinner.

Chilled Broccoli with Sauce Piquante

SERVES 8

2½ pounds fresh broccoli, cut lengthwise into attractive stalks
1   teaspoon salt
Water

Sauce Piquante:
⅓   cup dry white wine
3   scallions, sliced into ¼-inch pieces
1   teaspoon lemon juice
1½ cups mayonnaise (see p. 223)
½   teaspoon Dijon mustard
⅛   teaspoon curry powder
1   tablespoon finely chopped chives
Salt and ground black pepper to taste

Drop broccoli into boiling salted water; cook until just crisp tender (about 6 to 8 minutes). Rinse in cold water to stop cooking; drain on paper towels. Pat dry. Place broccoli in serving dish, stems pointing in and florets out. Set aside.

To make sauce: Combine white wine and scallions. Cook over medium heat until wine almost completely evaporates. Combine with remaining ingredients; season to taste. Pour over stems of broccoli. Refrigerate until serving.

Note: Sauce also good on cooked asparagus, cauliflower, etc.

Duck Breasts Calvados

SERVES 8

6   large duck breasts, skinned and boned (if
    using teal, allow at least 1 whole breast
    per person)
Salt and freshly ground pepper
12 tablespoons butter, divided
2   tart apples, peeled, cored, and thinly
    sliced (about 1½ cups)
2   tablespoons finely chopped shallots
½   cup Calvados
½   cup dry white wine
½   cup duck or chicken broth (see p. 221)

Season duck with salt and pepper. Melt
2 tablespoons butter in heavy skillet over
medium heat. Add duck breasts; brown
on all sides (about 3 minutes per side),
leaving them pink in center. Set aside to
keep warm.

Melt 2 tablespoons butter in same skillet.
Add apple slices; sauté until tender (about
5 minutes). Set aside to keep warm.

Melt 2 tablespoons butter in same skillet;
stir in shallots. Cook until tender and translucent. Add Calvados, wine, and stock to
deglaze skillet. Reduce liquid by one-half;
blend in remaining butter to thicken.

Slice duck breasts thinly, about same size
as apple slices. Arrange duck slices over apple slices. Cover with sauce.

Oven-Baked Herb Rice

SERVES 8

3   tablespoons butter, divided
1   medium onion, finely chopped (about ½
    cup)
2   cups rice
2   teaspoons salt, if using unsalted broth
⅛   teaspoon Cayenne pepper or 4 drops Ta-
    basco sauce
3   cups chicken broth (see p. 221)
Bouquet garni: 2 to 3 parsley sprigs, 1 bay
    leaf, and 4 sprigs fresh thyme or ½ tea-
    spoon dried thyme tied up in cheesecloth
    or garni bag

Preheat oven to 400°.

Heat 2 tablespoons butter in large, oven-
proof saucepan, 2½-quart capacity or
larger. Add onion; sauté until translucent.
Add rice; stir until grains are coated. Add
salt, pepper or Tabasco sauce, and chicken
broth. Place bouquet garni on top of rice.
Let rice broth mixture come to boil over
high heat. Cover; place in oven. Bake 17
minutes.* Remove from oven; uncover and
discard bouquet garni.

* For drier rice, cook 5 more minutes.

Kahlua-Mocha Mousse

SERVES 8 TO 12

½ cup Kahlua
½ cup dark crème de cacao
¾ cup strong brewed coffee
¾ teaspoon instant coffee granules
1   cup plus 2 tablespoons powdered sugar,
    divided
¼ teaspoon almond extract
1   envelope unflavored gelatin
7   eggs, separated
2   cups whipping cream, divided
Coffee granules or chocolate curls for garnish

Make collar around 1-quart soufflé dish with waxed paper. Set aside.

In top of double boiler, combine Kahlua, crème de cacao, coffee, coffee granules, 1 cup powdered sugar, almond extract, gelatin, and egg yolks. Mix well. Cook over boiling water (water should not touch bottom of double boiler), stirring until mixture thickens (10 to 15 minutes). Remove from heat.

Set top of double boiler in bowl of ice cubes; let stand, stirring occasionally until mixture thickens and makes mounds when dropped from spoon.

Meanwhile whip egg whites until stiff but not dry.

Chill cream, bowl, and beaters thoroughly. Whip 1½ cups cream until stiff. Fold egg whites and whipped cream into gelatin mixture. Pour mixture into prepared soufflé dish. Refrigerate until firm, preferably overnight.

Before serving, whip remaining cream with remaining powdered sugar until stiff. Put in pastry bag and decorate top. Sprinkle with coffee granules or chocolate curls.

WINTER MENU

for Ten

＊ Split Pea Soup

＊ Pork Roast with Cherry Glaze

Baked Yams with Butter

Spinach with Lemon Butter

＊ Radetzky Rice

Gewürztraminer or Côte de Rhone

Artist's Evening, *1916*
Lithograph by George Bellows
Museum purchase with funds provided by Mr. and Mrs. Alvin S. Romansky

Split Pea Soup

YIELDS 2½ QUARTS

Ham bone from baked ham or 3 ham hocks
8   cups water
1   pound split peas, washed
8   1-inch sprigs fresh thyme or ½ teaspoon
    dried thyme
3   1-inch sprigs fresh marjoram or ⅛ tea-
    spoon dried marjoram
½   teaspoon celery seed
2   cloves garlic, crushed
2   bay leaves
1   large carrot, chopped (about ⅔ cup)
1   large onion, chopped (about 1 cup)
½   teaspoon freshly ground pepper
1   10½-ounce can beef consommé
Salt to taste
1   pound ham, cut into ¼-inch cubes

Put ham bones and water in stock pot and simmer 1 hour, covered. Discard bones; strain stock and return to pot, adding water to make 8 cups. Add split peas, thyme, marjoram, celery seed, garlic, bay leaves, carrot, onion, pepper, and consommé. Simmer, covered, about 1¼ hours or until peas are very soft, almost falling apart.

Purée mixture. Taste, add salt as needed. Add diced ham. Heat and serve.

Note: When this soup is reheated it may need thinning with a little water.

Pork Roast with Cherry Glaze

SERVES 8 TO 10

5-pound boneless pork loin roast
½   teaspoon salt
½   teaspoon ground white pepper
1   cup cherry preserves
2   tablespoons light corn syrup
1   tablespoon red wine vinegar
¼   teaspoon ground cinnamon
¼   teaspoon ground cloves
¼   teaspoon grated nutmeg

Preheat oven to 500°.

Season roast with salt and pepper. Place roast fat side down in 9 × 13–inch pan. Roast 10 minutes. Reduce heat to 300°. Turn roast over with fat side up; continue roasting until meat thermometer registers 180° (about 1 hour).

For glaze, melt preserves in saucepan. Add other ingredients; mix well. Cook 5 minutes. During last 15 minutes of roasting, brush roast with cherry glaze. Remove roast from oven. Cover; let stand 30 minutes before serving.

Radetzky Rice

1½ cups rice
4 cups milk
¼ teaspoon salt
2 tablespoons butter
½ cup sugar
1 tablespoon lemon juice
Grated zest of ½ lemon
1 tablespoon orange juice
Grated zest of ½ orange
4 teaspoons rum
1 16-ounce can applesauce
4 to 6 ounces raspberry or strawberry jam
3 egg whites
2 tablespoons sugar
½ teaspoon vanilla extract (see p. 224)

Cook rice in milk with salt until tender. Strain.

Put butter, sugar, and lemon and orange juices and zest in heavy saucepan. Cook until sugar completely dissolves. Stir mixture into rice; mix well. Set aside to cool. Stir in rum.

Cook applesauce over low heat in heavy pan until it has reduced to 10 to 12 ounces.

Preheat oven to 450°.

Butter 12 4-ounce ramekins or 6-cup soufflé dish. Put layer of rice mixture on bottom. Spoon layer of jam over rice. Cover jam with layer of applesauce. Repeat layers of rice, jam, and applesauce until dish is filled.

Beat egg whites until frothy. Fold in sugar; beat until stiff. Add vanilla extract. Spread meringue over rice. Bake 15 minutes. Serve hot.

A CHINESE DINNER

for Six

*⋆White Cut Chicken

⋆Shredded Chicken Cold Dish

⋆Egg Drop Soup

⋆Five Star Anise Beef

⋆Chinese Fried Rice with Ham and Egg

⋆Mixed Chinese Vegetables

⋆Almond Float

Jasmine Tea or Beer*

The following Chinese menu features chicken poached in a manner typical of this cuisine. Although there are no salads in Chinese cuisine, the chicken meat may be used in a cold platter that is a close cousin to Western salads. The broth is delicious in soup. If the meal is to be served in Western fashion, start with the cold chicken platter, serve the soup next, and follow up with the beef, rice, and vegetables. If preferred, the chicken platter can be served with the main part of the meal. Dessert is light and satisfying to Western palates, although sweets are not typical of a Chinese meal.

*Two Mynahs, 1620
Hanging scroll by Wang Li
Gift of Mr. and Mrs. George Lenert Kroll*

White Cut Chicken

1   frying chicken (2½ to 3 pounds)
9   cups water
3   slices fresh gingerroot
2   tablespoons salt

Sauce:
4   tablespoons soy sauce
2   teaspoons toasted sesame seed oil*
Scallions or cilantro for garnish

Fold back chicken wings and place breast side down in large pot. Add water; chicken should be barely covered. Bring to boil, uncovered; skim off foam and scum. Add gingerroot slices and salt. Cover pot; lower heat to lowest setting; simmer 10 minutes. Turn off heat. DO NOT LIFT COVER!

Cool, covered, to room temperature, 4 to 5 hours. Remove chicken and drain well; refrigerate on platter until chilled with juices set.

Use in shredded chicken cold dish or serve as follows: chop chicken into serving-size pieces. Garnish with shredded scallions or cilantro, accompanied by sesame-soy sauce.

Note: Use broth for egg drop soup.
*Available in Chinese markets and specialty shops.

Shredded Chicken Cold Dish

SERVES 6 TO 8

1   whole cooked fryer (2½ to 3 pounds) or 2 whole cooked breasts
2   teaspoons Chinese mustard paste* (may substitute any hot mustard)
½   teaspoon five-spice powder* (may substitute allspice)
1   tablespoon toasted sesame seed oil*
1   teaspoon salt
3   tablespoons light soy sauce
Vegetable oil for frying
2   large squares egg roll skins or 8 small squares wonton skins
⅓   16-ounce package rice sticks*
½   head iceberg lettuce
¼   cup sliced toasted almonds
4   scallions, shredded
2   tablespoons finely chopped cilantro (optional)

Remove and discard chicken skin. Tear or cut meat into fine strips; place in bowl.

Mix mustard, five-spice powder, sesame seed oil, salt, and soy sauce. Add to chicken. Mix well.

Heat oil in deep-fat fryer to 400°. Cut egg roll skins into ⅛-inch strips; fry until light brown and crisp. Drain on absorbent paper.

Divide rice sticks into three batches; deep-fry each separately. Rice sticks expand immediately when placed in hot oil. Remove instantly. Drain.

Shred lettuce. Place on large platter. Layer chicken and egg roll strips and cover with fried rice sticks. Sprinkle with almonds, scallions, and cilantro. Just before serving, toss to combine.

*Available in Chinese markets and specialty shops.

Egg Drop Soup

SERVES 6

6   cups chicken broth from White Cut Chicken
2   teaspoons salt or to taste
2   tablespoons cornstarch
4   tablespoons water
2   eggs, lightly beaten
2   scallions, finely chopped

Bring broth to boil in saucepan. Add salt.

Mix cornstarch and water to make slurry. Add to broth; stir until it thickens and becomes clear. Pour in eggs slowly; stir once gently.

Remove from heat immediately. Add scallions. Serve at once.

Five Star Anise Beef

SERVES 6

2   tablespoons vegetable oil
4   slices fresh gingerroot
3   pounds boneless stewing beef, in 2-inch cubes, or whole beef shank
½   cup black soy sauce *
¼   cup dry sherry
3   tablespoons sugar
2   whole star anise pods (may substitute about 2 drops anise extract)
½-inch piece whole cinnamon
1   whole bunch scallions (8 to 10), cut into 5-inch lengths
1   cup water

Heat oil in wok or large heavy skillet over high heat. Add gingerroot and beef. Stir until all sides are brown and seared. Add soy sauce, sherry, sugar, anise, and cinnamon. Cook 5 minutes. Add scallions and water. Bring to boil; reduce heat to simmer. Cover; continue to cook 1 hour until beef is tender.

(Alternatively, use whole beef shanks, bone in. Cook as above, increasing final cooking time to 3 hours. It may be necessary to add more water during last 1½ hours. Cool cooked shank, slice thin, and serve cold in mixed platter or use in sandwiches.)

*Available in Chinese markets or specialty shops.

Chinese Fried Rice with Ham and Egg

SERVES 6 TO 8

6   tablespoons vegetable oil, divided
6   ounces smoked ham or 4 ounces boiled ham, chopped into small cubes
½   10-ounce package frozen peas
4   scallions, finely chopped
4   eggs, slightly beaten
6   cups cooked rice
3   teaspoons salt
½   teaspoon ground white pepper

Heat 1 tablespoon oil in wok or heavy skillet. Add ham; stir fry 2 minutes over moderate heat. Add peas, cook 1 minute. Set aside.

Heat remaining oil over high heat. Add scallions, stir 30 seconds. Add eggs; reduce heat to moderate. As soon as eggs form film in bottom of pan, add rice that has been fluffed with fork. Stir fry 2 to 3 minutes to mix eggs and rice. Add salt, pepper, ham, and peas. Stir fry 1 minute. Serve at once.

Mixed Chinese Vegetables

SERVES 6 TO 8

1   small head cauliflower
1   bunch broccoli
1   large carrot
3   tablespoons vegetable oil
1   tablespoon salt
3   tablespoons wood-ear, rehydrated (optional) *
1   16-ounce can whole miniature sweet corn ears, drained
1   teaspoon sugar
1   cup unsalted chicken broth (see p. 221)
2   tablespoons cornstarch
2   tablespoons water

Wash cauliflower; cut florets off stem and slice each floret into ¼-inch slices. Wash broccoli; cut florets off, peel skin if tough, and slice into ¼-inch slices. Peel carrot and cut diagonally into ¼-inch slices. Reserve cauliflower and broccoli stems for soups or slice into ¼-inch slices to add to stir-fry dishes.

Heat oil in wok or heavy skillet over high heat. Add salt, cauliflower, and carrots; stir fry 2 minutes. Add broccoli; stir fry 2 minutes. Add wood-ear, which has been soaked 30 minutes in warm water and drained, corn, sugar, and broth. When mixture boils, add cornstarch, which has been mixed with water to make slurry. Stir until clear glaze has formed around vegetables. Serve immediately.

*Available in Chinese markets or specialty shops.

Almond Float

SERVES 6 TO 8

2   envelopes (1 tablespoon each) unflavored gelatin
1¾ cups water, divided
½   cup sugar
1½ cups milk
1   tablespoon almond extract
1   16-ounce can mandarin oranges, chilled
1   1-pound can lychee nuts, chilled
8   Maraschino cherries

Soften gelatin in ½ cup water 5 minutes.

Bring remaining water to boil; add sugar and stir until dissolved. Add to softened gelatin; stir until clear. Add milk and almond extract. Pour mixture into flat 7½ × 12–inch dish. Refrigerate 4 hours until set.

Cut into diamond-shaped pieces. Serve in individual bowls with mandarin oranges, lychee nuts, and combined syrups. Garnish with cherries. For special touch, stuff lychee nuts with Maraschino cherries.

ONE-DISH SUPPER

for Eight

* Marinated Sunchokes

Greens and Cherry Tomatoes

* Chicken Tetrazzini

* Apricot Soufflé

Orvieto or Frascati

American Indian Jar, ca. 1880
Ceramic, Zuni Pueblo
Gift of Miss Ima Hogg

Marinated Sunchokes

SERVES 8

1   pound sunchokes (Jerusalem artichokes), peeled and thinly sliced
1   medium purple onion, thinly sliced (about ¾ cup)
½   cup olive oil
¼   cup white wine tarragon vinegar
1   teaspoon dry mustard
1   teaspoon dried Italian mixed herbs (oregano, marjoram, thyme, basil, rosemary, sage)
⅛   teaspoon freshly ground pepper
Salt to taste (optional)

Combine sunchokes and onion in 2-quart glass or ceramic container. Mix oil, vinegar, mustard, herbs, pepper, and salt in processor or blender. Blend; pour over vegetables; refrigerate overnight, turning occasionally.

May be used as salad or as part of composed salad. May be refrigerated for several days.

Chicken Tetrazzini

SERVES 8 TO 10

1   stewing chicken (4 to 5 pounds) or 4 pounds chicken breasts and 1 pound chicken thighs
1   teaspoon salt
1   large sprig parsley
1   bay leaf
1   rib celery with leaves, sliced
1   large onion, quartered
10 whole black peppercorns
3   whole cloves
Water to cover

Sauce:
1   pound fresh mushrooms, sliced (about 3 cups)
8   tablespoons butter, divided
6   tablespoons flour
3   cups chicken stock in which chicken was stewed
1   cup half-and-half
¾   cup vermouth or dry white wine
¾   cup shredded or grated Parmesan cheese, divided
3   tablespoons dry sherry
¼   cup finely chopped onion
⅛   teaspoon Tabasco sauce
½   teaspoon cracked black pepper or to taste
6   ounces vermicelli pasta
⅓   cup sliced almonds
1   tablespoon finely chopped parsley

In large pot place chicken, salt, parsley, bay leaf, celery, onion, peppercorns, and cloves. Cover with water. Bring to boil. Reduce heat; simmer until chicken is tender (20 to 30 minutes for pieces or 1 hour for whole chicken). Remove chicken; cool. Remove meat from bones; cut into bite-size pieces. Return bones but not skin to stock; simmer 1 hour. Cool; strain; skim fat off. Set aside.

Sauté mushrooms in 3 tablespoons butter and set aside.

Melt remaining butter; add flour. Blend until smooth. Add chicken stock, half-and-half, and vermouth. Blend until smooth and thickened. Remove from heat. Stir in ½ cup cheese, sherry, onion, Tabasco sauce, and pepper. Taste to correct seasoning. Reserve 1 cup sauce.

Cook pasta according to directions on package.

Preheat oven to 350°.

Fold chicken, mushrooms, and pasta into larger quantity sauce. Turn into 3-quart, oiled, shallow baking dish. Pour reserved cup of sauce evenly over mixture. Sprinkle with remaining cheese, almonds, and parsley. Dot with remaining butter. Bake until heated thoroughly and bubbling (20 to 30 minutes). Place under broiler to lightly brown.

Apricot Soufflé

SERVES 8 TO 10

1   6-ounce package dried apricots
1⅛ cups water
Grated zest of 1 lemon
1¼ cups sugar
5   eggs, separated
Juice of 1½ lemons
2   tablespoons butter
3   tablespoons flour
1½ cups milk
½   teaspoon salt
1   cup chopped walnuts

Preheat oven to 350°.

Place apricots in small, heavy saucepan with water. Bring to boil; simmer 20 minutes. Do not drain. Purée in processor or blender until smooth. Remove to large bowl.

Combine zest and sugar. Add to apricots. Add beaten egg yolks and lemon juice. Blend well.

Melt butter in heavy saucepan. Add flour; stir until smooth. Add milk; cook, stirring constantly until it reaches boil. Lower heat; simmer additional 1 minute, stirring constantly. Cool slightly; add to apricot mixture.

Beat egg whites with salt until stiff. Fold into mixture with walnuts. Spoon mixture into lightly buttered 2½-quart casserole. Place casserole in pan with hot water 1 inch deep. Bake 50 minutes. Serve immediately for hot soufflé. Upon standing, soufflé will fall but can be served as pudding at room temperature.

An Interior Scene, *1652*
Oil painting by Jan Molenaer
Gift of John H. McFadden, Jr.

FIRESIDE DINNER

for Two

* Italian Carrot Soup

* Indonesian Sate for Two

* Tomato Provençal

French Bread (see p. 143)

Cheese

* Velvet Hammer

Champagne

Italian Carrot Soup

YIELDS ABOUT 1½ QUARTS

4 tablespoons butter
1 medium onion, chopped (about ¾ cup)
4 large carrots, peeled and chopped (about 2 cups)
1 small turnip, peeled and chopped (about ⅓ cup)
12 coriander seeds, crushed
Salt to taste
Ground white pepper to taste
2 pints chicken broth (see p. 221)
¼ teaspoon dried marjoram
¼ teaspoon dried thyme
¼ teaspoon dried chervil

Garnish:
½ cup chopped fresh herbs, such as combination of chives, parsley, chervil, marjoram, and thyme

In heavy saucepan melt butter. Add onion, carrots, turnip, and coriander seeds. Season lightly with salt and pepper. Cover; simmer gently 20 minutes. Add chicken broth and herbs. Bring to boil; simmer 12 minutes. Purée in batches; return to saucepan; bring again to boil. Correct seasonings and consistency if necessary.

Indonesian Sate for Two

SERVES 2

½ pound pork loin, cut into 1½-inch pieces
½ teaspoon salt
⅛ teaspoon freshly ground pepper
2 teaspoons cumin seeds
½ cup vegetable oil
⅓ cup sliced onion
2 teaspoons brown sugar
2 tablespoons soy sauce
¾ teaspoon MSG (optional)
⅛ teaspoon ground ginger
½ to 1 cup cooked rice
2 limes, quartered

Combine pork, salt, pepper, cumin seeds, and oil in bowl. Meat should be completely covered with oil. Add onion, sugar, soy sauce, MSG, and ginger. Cover. Marinate 24 to 48 hours in refrigerator.

Drain meat; thread pieces on skewers. Broil 4 inches below flame 15 minutes, turning and basting with marinade. Pour remaining marinade, including onion, over hot rice. Serve skewered pork with limes.

Tomato Provençal

1   large tomato
⅛   teaspoon salt
⅛   teaspoon pepper
⅛   teaspoon dried sweet basil
⅛   teaspoon dried oregano
2   tablespoons butter
1   clove garlic, pressed

Cut tomato in half. Sprinkle salt, pepper, basil, and oregano on each half.

Melt butter; add garlic. Pour butter mixture on tomatoes. Let stand 1 hour.

Broil until slightly brown; then bake in 350° oven 8 to 10 minutes.

Velvet Hammer

6   scoops vanilla ice cream
2   ounces cognac
2   tablespoons banana liqueur
2   tablespoons orange liqueur

Place ingredients in blender; blend slowly until smooth. Serve in snifters.

Young Woman Peeling Potatoes, *ca. 1890*
Anonymous photograph
Museum purchase with funds provided by Mrs. Lucille Bowden Johnson

for Eight

Seasoned Tomato Juice

∗ Southern Fried Chicken with Cream Gravy

∗ Buttermilk Biscuits

∗ Purée of Winter Vegetables

∗ Beets in Horseradish Sauce

∗ Avocado and Grapefruit Mold Salad

∗ Yellow Squash Pickles

∗ Lemon Pound Cake

Grandmother offered an enormous "Sunday Dinner" in those gone-forever days when calories didn't count. This bountiful menu is suggested to bring back nostalgic memories of a lovely time in the past. However, modern-day tastes may prefer a menu of chicken, one vegetable, salad, and dessert. You be the judge.

Southern Fried Chicken with Cream Gravy

SERVES 8

2   frying chickens (2½ to 3 pounds each)
Salt
Ground black pepper
1   quart buttermilk
3   cups flour
5   tablespoons paprika
1   teaspoon Cayenne pepper
1½ teaspoons salt
3   teaspoons ground black pepper
Vegetable oil for frying

Cream Gravy:
8   tablespoons cooking oil in which chicken
    was fried
8   tablespoons seasoned flour left from
    dredging chicken
All brown bits left in oil from frying chicken
3   cups milk

Cut chickens into serving-size pieces. Pat dry with paper towels. Lightly sprinkle pieces with salt and black pepper. Dip each piece in buttermilk, turn to cover.

Combine flour, paprika, Cayenne pepper, salt, and pepper; mix well. Dip buttermilk-coated chicken into seasoned flour, one piece at a time.

Heat oil (¾ to 1 inch deep) in heavy iron skillet or in electric skillet to frying temperature (about 375°). Add chicken pieces. Do not crowd skillet so pieces will have crisp crust all over. Cook on one side until brown. Turn chicken. Cover; cook additional 15 to 20 minutes. Uncover; fry until crisp. Remove from skillet; drain on paper towels. Continue to fry in batches, keeping each batch warm in oven until all are cooked.

To make gravy: Remove all oil except 8 tablespoons from skillet. Stir in seasoned flour, scraping up browned bits. Cook, stirring, 2 minutes to make roux. Add cold milk and stir over medium heat until thickened. Taste to correct seasoning. Serve with chicken, potatoes, rice, or biscuits.

Buttermilk Biscuits

YIELDS 12 2½-INCH BISCUITS

2   cups flour
2½ teaspoons baking powder
¼   teaspoon baking soda
2   tablespoons solid vegetable shortening
1   cup buttermilk
⅛   teaspoon salt
½   teaspoon sugar (optional)

Sift flour, baking powder, and baking soda into bowl. Cut in shortening until it resembles coarse meal. Stir in buttermilk. Add salt and optional sugar. Cover dough; refrigerate 30 minutes.

Preheat oven to 375°.

Turn dough out on lightly floured board; pat, but do not roll, to ½-inch thickness. Cut with biscuit cutter; bake on ungreased cookie sheet 25 minutes or until lightly browned. Biscuits may also be dropped by tablespoonfuls onto ungreased cookie sheet and baked.

Purée of Winter Vegetables

SERVES 8

1½ pounds potatoes (all purpose)
1   large celeriac (celery root, celery rave,
    knob celery)
2   small firm turnips, pared and sliced
1   small onion, peeled and sliced
(Combined root vegetables should be
    1 pound)
1   teaspoon salt
½   teaspoon pepper
⅛   teaspoon grated nutmeg or less to taste
2   tablespoons butter

Peel and cube potatoes and celeriac. Cook together in boiling salted water until tender. Drain well.

Cook turnips and onion together in boiling salted water until tender. Drain well.

Place vegetables, seasonings, and butter in processor or blender in batches. Process until very smooth. Taste to adjust seasonings.

Beets in Horseradish Sauce

SERVES 8

1   cup sugar
1   cup white vinegar
1   cup liquid from beets
1   teaspoon salt
1   teaspoon finely chopped onion
1   tablespoon prepared horseradish
1   teaspoon grated orange zest
2   16-ounce jars small whole cooked beets
2   tablespoons cornstarch
¼   cup cold water
Finely chopped chives (optional)

In large saucepan combine first 7 ingredients. Bring to boil; lower heat and simmer 5 minutes. Add beets and simmer additional 5 minutes. Remove beets from liquid and keep warm.

Dissolve cornstarch in water; stir into seasoned liquid. Cook, stirring, until thickened and clear.

Place beets in serving dish. Pour 1 cup sauce over beets. Garnish with finely chopped chives.

Avocado and Grapefruit Mold Salad

SERVES 8

1   large grapefruit
2   envelopes unflavored gelatin
¾   cup orange juice
Juice from grapefruit plus enough frozen or canned juice to make 1 cup
½   teaspoon salt
¼   cup lemon juice
1   teaspoon grated orange zest
1   teaspoon grated lemon zest
½   cup sour cream
¼   teaspoon Tabasco sauce or to taste
1   large avocado
4   egg whites
⅓   cup sugar
Lettuce for garnish

Peel and section grapefruit, removing all pith and membranes.

Soften gelatin in orange juice.

Heat grapefruit juice but do not boil. Add to softened gelatin; stir to dissolve completely. Add salt, lemon juice, and zests. Cool slightly. Gradually stir in sour cream and Tabasco sauce. Chill to consistency of unbeaten egg white (20 to 30 minutes).

Meanwhile, peel avocado and cut into ½-inch cubes. Mix with grapefruit sections.

Beat egg whites until frothy. Gradually add sugar; beat until stiff, shiny peaks form.

Into partially set gelatin mixture, fold grapefruit and avocado. Fold in egg whites. Pour into 6-cup mold or 8 individual molds. Chill several hours or until set. Serve on lettuce leaves.

Yellow Squash Pickles

YIELDS 5 PINTS

2   pounds yellow squash, thinly sliced (about 8 cups)
3   large onions, thinly sliced (about 3 cups)
2   tablespoons pickling salt
2   cups white vinegar
2   large green bell peppers, chopped (about 2 cups)
2   cups sugar
2   teaspoons celery seed
2   teaspoons mustard seed

Combine squash and onions in bowl; sprinkle with salt. Let stand 1 hour. Drain well.

Mix vinegar, pepper, sugar, and seeds. Bring to boil and boil 1 minute. Add well-drained squash and onions; return to boil and boil 2 minutes. Pack into sterilized jars and seal.

Lemon Pound Cake

SERVES 14 TO 16

3   cups flour
⅛   teaspoon salt
½   pound butter
3   cups sugar
4   large eggs
Grated zest of 1 large lemon
1   tablespoon fresh lemon juice
1   teaspoon vanilla extract (see p. 224)
¼   teaspoon baking soda
1   cup buttermilk
Powdered sugar (optional)

Sift flour and salt together; set aside.

Cream butter and sugar until light and fluffy. Add eggs, one at a time, mixing thoroughly after each addition. Add lemon zest, lemon juice, and vanilla extract, mixing thoroughly. Add baking soda to buttermilk. Then add flour and buttermilk alternately to butter-sugar-egg mixture, always beginning and ending with flour.

Butter and sugar 9½-inch Bundt pan. Spoon in batter, cutting through in several places to release any large air pockets.

Place in cold oven; turn on heat to 350° and bake about 1 hour or until cake tester comes out dry. Cool in pan 10 minutes before turning out on rack. May be dusted with powdered sugar if desired.

Note: 1 cup chopped pecans, walnuts, or almonds may be added to batter or layered in batter.

MEXICAN BRUNCH

for Six

＊Mimosas

＊Chilaquiles (Mexican Scrambled Eggs)

＊Tortillas de Harina Fronterizas (Flour Tortillas)

＊Buttermilk Pecan Pralines

＊Cafe de Olla (Mexican Coffee)

[Mexico], *n.d.*
Photograph by Edward Steichen
Bequest of Edward Steichen by direction of Joanna T. Steichen and George Eastman House

Mimosas

SERVES 6

1   bottle Asti Spumanti, well chilled
4   cups freshly squeezed orange juice,
    strained and chilled
Fresh strawberries

In pitcher combine Asti Spumanti and orange juice. Stir mixture once. Serve in chilled champagne glasses with fresh strawberry.

Variation: For nonalcoholic Mimosas, substitute dry ginger ale for Asti Spumanti.

Chilaquiles
(Mexican Scrambled Eggs)

SERVES 6

3 to 4 tablespoons corn oil, divided
1   large onion, chopped (about 1 cup)
½   green bell pepper, chopped
1 to 2 jalapeños, finely chopped, or to taste
1   clove garlic, pressed
12 corn tortillas
12 eggs
½   cup milk

Heat 1 tablespoon oil in large skillet; sauté onion, pepper, jalapeños, and garlic until soft. Remove from skillet; set aside.

Cut tortillas into eighths.

Heat remaining oil. Fry tortillas in small quantities until they begin to stiffen. Add more oil if necessary. Remove; drain on paper towels.

Beat eggs and add milk. Cook on moderate heat until soft. Add onion-pepper mixture; fold tortillas into eggs. Cook to desired consistency.

Serve with the following condiments: chopped tomatoes, sliced avocados, chopped fresh cilantro, chopped scallions, salsa piquante,* and red pepper sauce (see p. 223).

*Available in most supermarkets and Mexican specialty shops.

Tortillas de Harina Fronterizas
(Flour Tortillas)

YIELDS 12

2   cups flour
1   teaspoon salt
½   cup lard
¼   cup cold water

Place flour and salt in mixing bowl. Cut in lard with pastry blender or fork until consistency of coarse meal. Add water, a little at a time, until dough forms ball. Make 1¼-inch balls. Roll on lightly floured board as thin as possible.

Place on hot griddle. Cook 2 or 3 minutes or until slightly brown, turning once. Cover; set aside until ready to serve. Steam over boiling water before serving. Wrap in tea towel to keep warm.

Buttermilk Pecan Pralines

YIELDS 30 TO 32 2-INCH PIECES

2   cups light brown sugar or 2 cups granu-
    lated sugar
1   cup buttermilk
⅛   teaspoon salt
2½ cups pecan halves
2½ tablespoons butter

Mix together sugar, buttermilk, and salt in heavy saucepan. Cook, stirring constantly, until soft-ball stage (236°; about 5 minutes).

Pour into large mixing bowl. Add pecan halves and butter. Stir just to mix in nuts and melt butter. Cool slightly. Beat with wooden spoon until mixture is creamy or looks lighter in color and more opaque. Drop by teaspoonfuls onto waxed paper.

Cafe de Olla
(Mexican Coffee)

SERVES 6

8   cups cold water
½   cup plus 2 tablespoons ground coffee
½   cup dark brown sugar
2   sticks cinnamon

In large saucepan heat water to boil. Add all ingredients. Return to boil, continuing to boil 1 minute. Remove from heat. Strain and serve in small cups.

Untitled, ca. 1932
Photograph by Albert Renger-Patzch
Museum purchase with funds provided by Mr. and Mrs. Harry B. Gordon

for Eight

⋆ Apple Liver Pâté

French Bread (see p. 143)

⋆ Sopa de Guadalajara over Rice

⋆ Chocolate Truffle Pie

Hot Coffee with Rum and Cinnamon Stick

Pinot Noir or Petite Sirah

Texas is little known for snow-clad mountains complete with ski resorts. However, undaunted by such mundane considerations, an increasing number of Texan ski enthusiasts make an annual pilgrimage to neighboring states to pursue the exhilarating sport. After a day on the slopes, weary and hungry skiers will enjoy a hearty meal with plenty of calories to burn off the next day.

Apple Liver Pâté

YIELDS 3 CUPS

12 tablespoons butter, divided
1   medium onion, finely chopped (about ½ cup)
1   medium apple, peeled, cored, chopped, and sprinkled with juice of ½ lemon (about ½ cup)
1   pound chicken livers, rinsed and drained
⅓   cup applejack or brandy
1   teaspoon salt
Pepper to taste
⅛   teaspoon ground allspice or to taste

In medium skillet melt 1 tablespoon butter. Sauté onion until soft. Add apple and cook 2 minutes. Place in processor or blender.

In same skillet melt 2 tablespoons butter. Sauté chicken livers until cooked but slightly pink in centers. Add applejack and flame. Add to onion-apple mixture. Process until smooth.

Beat remaining butter until soft. Add liver mixture to butter; add salt, pepper, and allspice; mix until creamy. Put in crock. Seal with clarified butter if desired or cover with plastic wrap. Chill overnight.

Let stand 1 hour at room temperature before serving. May be frozen.

Sopa de Guadalajara over Rice

YIELDS 16 TO 18 CUPS

3½ to 4 pounds boneless pork shoulder
1   tablespoon vegetable oil
1   large onion, finely chopped (about 1 cup)
3   cloves garlic, finely chopped
1   tablespoon chili powder
1   tablespoon finely chopped jalapeño chilies (optional)
2   teaspoons chopped fresh oregano or 1 teaspoon dried oregano
1   teaspoon cumin seed
6   cups water
2   10½ ounce cans beef broth
1   cup dried pinto or small red beans
4   large carrots, thinly sliced (about 4 cups)
3   ears fresh corn (about 1½ cups kernels) or 2 4-ounce jars baby corn on the cob, drained
Salt to taste
Pepper to taste

Trim excess fat from meat; cut meat into 1- to 1½-inch cubes. In 5-quart heavy saucepan, heat oil over medium-high heat. Add meat; brown well on all sides. Remove from saucepan.

In same saucepan add onion and garlic; sauté until limp. Stir in chili powder, optional jalapeño, oregano, cumin seed, water, beef broth, and beans. Add meat. Cover; simmer about 1½ hours or until meat and beans are tender. Cover and refrigerate. When chilled, skim fat from broth and discard.

Heat broth to boiling; add carrots. Cover and simmer 30 minutes or until carrots are tender. Stir in corn. Taste to determine amount of salt and pepper to add. (Canned beef broth is salted.) Cook until fresh corn is tender or canned corn is thoroughly heated. Pour into tureen. Serve over cooked brown rice with following condiments: halved cherry tomatoes, chopped scallions including green tops, chopped fresh coriander, sour cream, lime wedges, chopped fresh jalapeño chilies or bottled jalapeño sauce, and chopped avocado.

Chocolate Truffle Pie

SERVES 6 TO 8

Crust:

4 tablespoons butter
1 7-ounce package angel flake coconut
¼ teaspoon salt

Filling:

12 tablespoons butter
¾ cup sugar
2 ounces unsweetened chocolate, melted
4 eggs
1 cup chopped pecans
¼ teaspoon salt
2 teaspoons vanilla extract (see p. 224)

To make crust: Melt butter. Add coconut and brown over medium heat. Add salt. Pour into 10-inch pie pan. Pat into shell. Cool.

To make filling: Melt butter; add sugar and cream well. Add melted chocolate; mix well. Add eggs, one at a time, beating 5 minutes after addition of each egg. Add pecans, salt, and vanilla extract. Pour into prepared shell. Chill in refrigerator at least 4 hours or in freezer 30 minutes.

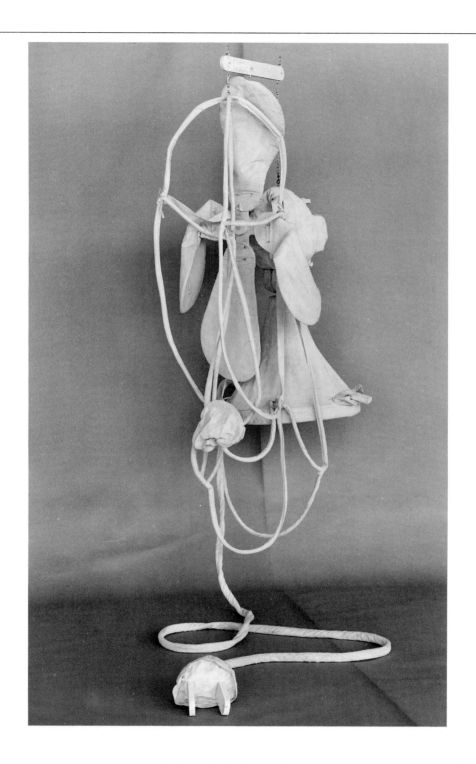

Giant Soft Fan, Ghost Version, *1967*
Canvas, wood, and foam rubber by Claes Oldenburg
Gift of Dominique and John de Menil

214

BASICS AND BONUSES

Some Cake Equivalents

Two 8-inch rounds	= two thin 8 × 8 × 2–inch squares
	= one 12 × 8 × 2–inch rectangle
	= twenty-four 2½-inch cupcakes
Two 9-inch rounds	= two 8 × 8 × 2–inch squares
	= one 15 × 10 × 1–inch rectangle
	= one 13 × 9 × 2–inch rectangle
	= thirty 2½-inch cupcakes
One 10-inch tube pan	= two 9 × 5 × 3–inch loaves
	= one 15 × 10 × 1–inch rectangle
	= one 13 × 9 × 2–inch rectangle
	= thirty 2½-inch cupcakes
One 9 × 5 × 3–inch loaf	= one 9 × 9 × 2–inch square
	= twenty-four 2½-inch cupcakes

Other Equivalents

3 teaspoons = 1 tablespoon
1 fluid ounce = 2 tablespoons
1 cup = 16 tablespoons
1 pound flour = 4 cups
1 pound sugar = 2 cups
¼ pound butter = 8 tablespoons

8 egg whites = 1 cup
16 egg yolks = 1 cup
¼ pound cheese = about 1 cup, grated
1 pound shrimp, jumbo = about 18
     large = about 22
     medium = about 30 to 35
     small = over 35

Approximate Metric Conversions of Liquid Measurements

¼ c (4 TB)	2 oz	.5 dl (59 ml)
⅓ c (5 TB)	2⅔ oz	.75 dl (79 ml)
½ c	4 oz	1 dl (119 ml)
⅔ c	5⅓ oz	1.5 dl (157 ml)
1 c	8 oz	.25 L (237 ml)
1½ c	12 oz	.35 L (355 ml)
1¾ c	14 oz	.40 L (414 ml)
2 c (1 pt)	16 oz	.5 L (473 ml)
4 c (2 pt; 1 qt)	32 oz	1 L (946 ml)

c = cup
pt = pint
qt = quart
TB = tablespoon

oz = liquid ounce

dl = deciliter
L = liter
ml = milliliter

Note: Exact conversions: quarts × .095 = liters.

Miscellaneous Hints

Boiling and Scalding:

When boiling cabbage, broccoli, Brussels sprouts, and other strong vegetables, add a bay leaf to the water to neutralize the aroma.

When boiling pasta, rice, or potatoes, add a teaspoon of butter or oil to the water to keep it from boiling over.

When scalding milk or cream rinse the pan first in cold water to minimize sticking and to enable the pan to be cleaned more easily.

Cheese:

Melt cheese over low heat. High heat causes it to become stringy.

To keep cheese fresh over an extended period of time, wrap it in vinegar-soaked cheesecloth and refrigerate in a plastic bag.

Eggs:

When hard boiling eggs, put a small hole in the round end with a pin to allow for air expansion as the egg cooks. This will prevent the egg from cracking as it boils.

To center the yolk in hard-boiled eggs, rotate them several times in the water before it comes to a boil.

Eggs should be at room temperature for cookery. Whites will mount higher when whipped and yolks will be incorporated more easily into sauces and doughs.

Egg whites may be frozen "as is." Mark packages as to quantity and date.

Egg yolks may be frozen if stabilized with either salt or sugar in the ratio of a pinch of salt per yolk or 1/8 teaspoon sugar per yolk. Mark container as to quantity, date, and stabilizer. Use within 6 weeks for mayonnaise, hollandaise, or a sweet sauce.

Herbs:

A scant teaspoon of dried herb is equal to about 1½ tablespoons of fresh herb.

Soak dried herbs in oil, wine, or hot water before using to bring out the aromatic oils.

Measuring:

When measuring solid vegetable shortening, fill the measure first with an amount of cold water to make a *cup* when added to the shortening. Add shortening until the water reaches the 1-cup line.

Before measuring sticky liquids, oil the cup with vegetable oil and rinse with hot water.

See also "Measurements and Definitions," p. 8.

Mexican Foods:

Mexican cuisine always uses white onions.

Mexican cuisine uses lard for frying and sautéing.

Pastry and Cakes:

Butter or shortening should be very cold for making pastry. Let the dough "rest" in the refrigerator for about an hour before rolling it out. This allows the gluten to relax and the butter to firm up again and produces a flakier crust.

Cool baked filled pies on a cake rack to keep the bottom crust crisp.

When making cakes, all ingredients should be at room temperature.

Peeling and Shelling:

To peel bell peppers or fresh chilies, roast over gas flame or broil under flame or electric broiler until they are charred and blistered, turning for even exposure to heat. Place in a plastic bag, tightly closed, and allow them to sweat for 15 minutes. Peel skin under running water. Slice and rinse seeds away. Be sure to wear rubber gloves when handling hot chilies.

Tomatoes, peaches, and nectarines peel easily when plunged for a few seconds into boiling water and then immediately into iced water to stop cooking.

For ease in shelling nuts, bake at 350° for 15 minutes or boil for 15 minutes before shelling.

Shortcuts:

Quick soak for beans: wash, cover with 3 inches water, bring to boil, boil 2 minutes, remove from heat, let stand 1 hour, uncovered, to absorb water. Cook as usual.

Shortcut for cooking meatballs: place uncooked 1¼-inch meat balls on ungreased rimmed baking sheet. Cover with paper and chill in refrigerator until ready to use. Bake in hot oven 8 to 11 minutes. Outside will be brown, inside pink. Add to preheated sauce so that meatballs will not continue cooking. Adjust time according to size ball.

Storage:

Freeze fish or shrimp covered with water in cartons to maintain maximum fresh taste.

Garlic cloves may be stored in a jar of olive oil or vegetable oil. This keeps the garlic from drying out and makes a good garlic-flavored oil for dressings.

Store whole lemons in the refrigerator in a tightly sealed jar of water. The juice yield will be almost doubled. Or submerge in hot water for 15 minutes before squeezing.

Store onions in the refrigerator to minimize "tears" while chopping.

Rinse chopped onions in a colander under hot water to wash away volatile oils. This whitens them, gives a milder taste, and enables them to be stored in the refrigerator for several days keeping a fresh taste and appearance.

Start a stockpot bag for the freezer. Freeze bones, tomato skins, carrot ends, extra onion pieces, and so on. Add to pot when making stock.

STOCKS, SAUCES, AND SOUPS

Basic Stocks

In preparing stock, make as much as will fill a very large stockpot. Freeze it in small portions. You will enjoy having good homemade stock on hand whenever needed. It will keep 2 or 3 days in the refrigerator but must be reboiled after that time and again every 2 days.

After the stock has been cooked, strained, chilled, and completely defatted, it may be reduced over high heat to make a glaze. This concentrates the flavor and takes less storage space. Reduce 1 quart of stock to 1 cup of glaze. Cool it, cut it into cubes, and freeze it. The glaze is a wonderful enrichment to sauces, stews, and soups. It also makes an excellent hot dressing for steamed vegetables or baked potatoes (melt a small cube directly on the hot vegetables). It may be reconstituted by adding water to regain "stock" consistency.

In the process of reducing stock to a glaze or a stronger stock, the ratio of salt to liquid is greatly increased. Therefore, stock should not be salted until you are ready to use it.

Stock may be used to poach chicken, fish, or meat. For example, use chicken stock to poach chicken pieces or a whole chicken. The taste of the chicken will be superb and the stock will be further enriched. It is then called a "double stock." It may be used again for poaching more chicken, thus becoming a "triple stock," and so on.

Brown Stock

YIELDS ABOUT 4 QUARTS

6 to 8 pounds beef and veal bones, including veal knuckle bone cut in half; bones should have substantial amount of meat
4 to 6 carrots, sliced
2 large onions, sliced
4 leeks, sliced
2 ribs celery, sliced
1 large tomato, halved and seeded but not skinned
1 turnip, sliced
10 peppercorns
Bouquet garni (see pp. 43 and 185)
Water to cover (about 5 quarts)

Preheat oven to 425°.

Place all bones in large shallow pan; brown in oven until dark but not burned. Remove from oven. Pour off fat, saving about 2 tablespoons. Deglaze pan; scrape brown bits. Set aside. Put reserved fat in large skillet; brown carrots and onions, stirring to prevent burning. Pour off excess fat.

Combine browned meat with deglazed juices, vegetables, and remaining ingredients in large stockpot. Bring to boil; immediately reduce heat to simmer. Cook about 8 hours, skimming as necessary. Add water to maintain same level of liquid. Strain through sieve lined with wet cheesecloth. Refrigerate overnight; remove fat. Stock is ready to use or to be reduced to glaze.

Court Bouillon

YIELDS 2 QUARTS

1 carrot, chopped
1 rib celery with leaves, chopped
½ small onion, sliced
1 bay leaf
1 teaspoon white peppercorns
1 cup dry white wine
3 or 4 sprigs parsley
2 quarts water

Mix all ingredients in stainless steel or enamel saucepan. Bring to boil. Reduce to simmer and cook 1 to 2 minutes. Use to poach fish.

In large heavy stockpot, melt butter. Add carrots, onions, scallions, and celery. Cover and cook until vegetables are soft. Add remaining ingredients; simmer, partially covered, about 2 hours. Strain through fine sieve lined with wet cheesecloth. Stock may be kept in refrigerator several days or divided among small jars and frozen.

Fumet
(Fish Stock)

YIELDS 1¾ QUARTS

1	tablespoon butter
1	medium onion, sliced
½	carrot, sliced
3	pounds fish frames and heads
1	cup dry white wine or dry vermouth
6	peppercorns
1	large bay leaf
6 to 8	stems parsley
⅛	teaspoon thyme
2	quarts water

In large pot, melt butter; add onion and carrot. Cover; cook until vegetables are soft. Add remaining ingredients; bring just to boil. Reduce heat; simmer, uncovered, 30 to 35 minutes. Strain through sieve lined with wet cheesecloth. Refrigerate until fat rises to top. Remove fat. If stronger flavor is desired, increase amount of heads and bones.

White Stock

YIELDS ABOUT 4 QUARTS

6 to 8	pounds veal bones or veal and chicken bones, including veal knuckle bone cut in half
4	large carrots, sliced
2	large onions, chopped
4	leeks, sliced
2	ribs celery, sliced
2 to 4	scallions, chopped (optional)
	Bouquet garni (see pp. 43 and 185)
10	peppercorns
	Water to cover (about 5 quarts)

In large stockpot, place bones and cover with water. Bring to boil. Pour off water and resultant scum. Wash bones and return to pot. Add remaining ingredients; cover with water and bring to boil. Reduce heat to simmer; continue to simmer about 8 hours, uncovered. Simmer should be one in which water barely moves. Remove scum as necessary. Add more water to maintain same amount of liquid. Strain through sieve lined with wet cheesecloth. Refrigerate overnight. Remove fat from top. Stock is ready to use or may be reduced to glaze.

Note: Chicken stock is made in the same way, using giblets and bones but *not* liver, which will make cloudy, liver-tasting stock.

Vegetable Stock

YIELDS 1½ QUARTS

1	tablespoon butter
3	carrots, sliced
2	large onions, sliced
2 to 4	scallions, including green tops, sliced
1	small rib celery with leaves, sliced
1	small tomato, halved and seeded but not skinned
	Bouquet garni (see pp. 43 and 185)
2	quarts water

Crème Fraîche

YIELDS 1 CUP

1   cup heavy cream
1   tablespoon sour cream

Mix creams in scalded jar. Cover loosely. Let stand at room temperature 8 to 24 hours, depending on temperature of room. Stir. Refrigerate. It will thicken on being refrigerated.

Grape Sauce

YIELDS 1½ CUPS

½   cup grape jelly
½   cup catsup
½   cup butter
1   teaspoon ground cinnamon
1   teaspoon ground allspice

Cook jelly, catsup, and butter in saucepan over low heat until melted. Add cinnamon and allspice. Sauce may be served with lamb, ham, or pork.

Herb Butter

¼   pound butter
2   tablespoons chopped fresh herb
⅛   teaspoon salt
3 to 4   drops fresh lemon juice

Soften butter. Add rest of ingredients, mix well. Shape into roll, wrap in plastic wrap, chill thoroughly or freeze. Slice as needed to dress vegetables, fish, or meat. Use as spread on sandwiches and canapes.
Suggested herbs:
For fish: dill, chives, tarragon
For vegetables: basil, oregano, marjoram, parsley
For meats: rosemary, chives

Hollandaise Sauce

YIELDS ABOUT 2 CUPS

¼   cup water plus 2 tablespoons, divided
1   tablespoon lemon juice or white wine vinegar
½   teaspoon salt
⅛   teaspoon ground white pepper
3   egg yolks
½   pound butter, melted

Mix ¼ cup water with lemon juice or vinegar, salt, and pepper in heavy saucepan. Cook over high heat to reduce liquid to 1½ to 2 tablespoons. Remove from heat; cool mixture slightly. Add egg yolks; whisk over very low heat until mixture is thick. Remove from heat. Add warm (not hot) melted butter a little at a time, alternating with remaining water. Whisk constantly to form emulsion. Strain, correct seasoning, and keep warm over hot (not boiling) water. Sauce must not be heated beyond 180° in order to prevent egg yolk from scrambling and making sauce unusable.

Note: If sauce separates because of standing a long time, add 1 or 2 teaspoons boiling water. Whisk vigorously and it will re-emulsify. To stabilize, add tablespoon of Béchamel (see p. 224) or cream sauce or combine ½ teaspoon cornstarch and ½ cup water. Cook until thick; add 1 tablespoon mixture to hollandaise. Stabilized sauce will not separate.

Mayonnaise

YIELDS ABOUT 1½ CUPS

1   egg yolk
¼   teaspoon salt
⅛   teaspoon ground white pepper
1   teaspoon Dijon mustard (optional)
2   tablespoons vinegar, lemon juice, or
    combination of both
1   cup oil
1   tablespoon hot water

In shallow bowl, beat egg yolk with salt, pepper, mustard, and vinegar. Add oil by drops, beating constantly, until emulsion forms. Add remaining oil by spoonfuls; continue beating until all oil is used. Stir in hot water to stabilize mixture. Mayonnaise will be thin but will thicken after being refrigerated.

Variation: Use flavored vinegars or oils of different flavors or add chopped fresh herbs to finished mayonnaise.

Note: If emulsion breaks and mayonnaise separates, it may be "rescued" by allowing it to stand until completely separated. Skim oil from top. Set aside. Beat one egg yolk; add curdled yolk bit by bit until emulsion forms. Add removed oil; continue until mayonnaise is finished.

Pesto

YIELDS ABOUT 1½ CUPS

1   cup olive oil
⅓   cup pine nuts
2 to 3 cloves garlic
1   cup fresh basil leaves
⅓   cup grated Parmesan or Romano cheese
    or combination of both
⅓   teaspoon salt

Combine all ingredients in blender or processor. Blend until basil leaves are almost puréed. Pour into small containers. Allow oil to come to top to completely cover puréed ingredients. If there is not enough oil to cover ingredients by at least ¼ inch in containers, add additional oil. Use on pasta or vegetables (cooked eggplant, zucchini, tomatoes, artichokes). Use sparingly at first since pesto has strong taste. May be refrigerated for several weeks or frozen up to 6 months.

Red Pepper Sauce

YIELDS ABOUT 6 CUPS

4   red bell peppers (about 2 cups)
1   large onion, sliced (about 3 cups)
¼   cup olive oil
2 or 3 ripe tomatoes, peeled and cut into
    wedges (about 2 cups)
Salt to taste
Pepper to taste

Put peppers under broiler 2 to 3 inches from heat until skin blisters. Keep turning until all sides are charred. Place in plastic bag 10 minutes. Peel, seed, and cut lengthwise into thin strips.

Cut onion into ½-inch slices and quarter. Sauté in oil until soft. Add peppers and tomatoes and sauté briefly. Add salt and pepper to taste. Vegetables should retain shape. Serve with scrambled eggs, grits, pork chops, quail, or dove. Good cold on sourdough bread as lunch dish.

Roux-Based Sauces

The most famous of roux-based sauces is Béchamel, which is used as a base for many other sauces. The method for making all roux-based sauces is basically the same. Proportions of flour and butter to liquid produce sauces of various thicknesses. Amounts are determined by the ultimate use in a recipe. Proportions are as follows:

Soups:
1 tablespoon flour
1 tablespoon butter
1 cup liquid

Sauces:
2 tablespoons flour
2 tablespoons butter
1 cup liquid

Soufflés:
3 tablespoons flour
3 tablespoons butter
1 cup liquid

Liquid may be milk (plain or seasoned), cream, stock, or combination. When sauce is made with chicken, veal, or fish stock, it is known as "velouté."

Béchamel Sauce:
1 cup milk
1 bay leaf
1 slice onion
2 cloves
2 tablespoons butter
2 tablespoons flour
Salt to taste
Pepper to taste
Grated nutmeg to taste

In small saucepan, heat milk with bay leaf, onion, and cloves. Bring just to boil. Remove from heat; allow to cool to tepid.

In heavy pan melt butter. Add flour and cook 2 minutes, stirring constantly. Pour milk through strainer into roux. Stir until mixture thickens. Season with salt, pepper, and nutmeg to taste. Strain.

Vanilla Extract

YIELDS 1 PINT

1 ounce (about 6) whole vanilla beans, cut lengthwise into 4 pieces
1 pint brandy or vodka

Combine vanilla beans and brandy in jar—preferably brown glass liquor bottle. Seal with cap or stopper. Shake. For best flavor, let mixture age about 6 months. As it ages, mixture darkens. Leave beans in mixture, adding additional brandy as vanilla is used. Homemade extract may be used full strength in any recipe calling for vanilla extract.

Vinaigrette

YIELDS 1 CUP

¼ cup acid, such as lemon juice, vinegar, or combination
½ teaspoon salt
½ small clove garlic, pressed (optional)
¾ cup oil

Combine acid, salt, and garlic in jar. Shake until salt dissolves. Add oil and shake to emulsify.

Variation: Use different acids of flavored vinegars, lemon juice, dry sherry, vermouth, red or white wine, any of which may be diluted with a little water. The oil may be vegetable, olive, walnut, or combination. Chopped herbs, mustards of various types, freshly cracked pepper, or chopped shallots add flavor and variety.

Flavored Vinegars

Fruit Flavors:
Fresh or frozen unsweetened raspberries, blueberries, or blackberries
White wine vinegar, rice wine vinegar, or distilled vinegar diluted with a little water

Fill jar with fruit. Cover fruit completely with vinegar. Let stand at room temperature several days, up to 1 week. Strain off fruit-flavored vinegar.

Herb Flavors:
Washed and dried herb, such as tarragon, basil, mint, or dill
Cider vinegar, red wine vinegar, or white wine vinegar

Place generous bunch of herb in clean jar. Heat vinegar to boiling, pour over herb, cover loosely. Let stand several days at room temperature to develop flavor before using. Add fresh vinegar to replace herb-flavored vinegar as it is used.

Broccoli Soup

SERVES 6

1 large bunch broccoli, washed, stemmed, and broken into florets or 2 10-ounce packages frozen broccoli florets
3½ cups strong chicken stock (see p. 221)
1 medium onion, quartered
2 tablespoons butter
1 teaspoon salt (less if using canned broth)
¼ teaspoon freshly ground pepper
2 teaspoons curry powder
2 tablespoons lime juice or to taste
8 thin lemon or lime slices for garnish
½ cup sour cream for garnish
1 tablespoon chopped chives for garnish

In large saucepan, combine broccoli, chicken stock, onion, butter, salt, and pepper. Add enough broth to curry powder to make smooth thin paste. Add to pan. Heat to boiling. Reduce heat; simmer 12 minutes.

Purée mixture in blender or processor, one-half at a time. Pour into bowl; stir in lime juice. Cover; refrigerate at least 4 hours. Serve in small bowls, garnished with lime or lemon slices, sour cream, and chives.

Variation: 2 10-ounce packages of frozen chopped spinach, thawed and drained, may be substituted for broccoli.

Cioppino

SERVES 8

½ cup olive oil
2 large onions, cut into wedges
2 bunches scallions, including tops, chopped (about 2 to 3 cups)
2 green bell peppers, seeded and chopped (about 1¼ cups)
4 large cloves garlic, finely chopped
4 cups water
2 cups red or white wine
1 1-pound, 12-ounce can tomatoes, chopped, with juice
1 bay leaf
1 teaspoon dried oregano
1 teaspoon dried basil
⅔ cup chopped parsley
1 tablespoon salt
1 tablespoon sugar
2 pounds lump crab meat
2 pounds shrimp, cleaned and deveined

Sauté onions, scallions, green pepper, and garlic in olive oil 5 minutes. Add water and wine; simmer. Add tomatoes, herbs, and seasonings. Cover; simmer 1 hour. Add crab meat; simmer 5 minutes. Add shrimp; simmer 10 minutes. Serve over rice.

Iced Crab Soup

1   quart buttermilk
1   teaspoon salt
1   teaspoon sugar
1   teaspoon dry mustard or to taste
2   teaspoons water
1   cup chopped peeled cucumber
1½ tablespoons chopped fresh dill or 2 teaspoons dry dill
1   cup fresh lump crab meat
Slices of unpeeled cucumber for garnish
Paprika for garnish

Mix buttermilk, salt, and sugar. Mix mustard and water to form paste and add to buttermilk mixture. Add all other ingredients and chill several hours before serving. Garnish with thin slice of unpeeled cucumber sprinkled with paprika.

Oyster, Brie, and Champagne Soup

½   pound butter
½   cup flour
2   quarts fish stock (see p. 221)
5   cups milk
1¾ pounds Brie cheese
1½ teaspoons red pepper
3   dozen fresh oysters
1   cup finely chopped scallions, including green tops
2   cups brut champagne
Salt to taste

Melt butter and stir in flour. Cook on low heat 3 minutes, stirring constantly. Slowly add stock while stirring and cook 4 minutes on moderate heat. Bring to boil. Lower heat and simmer 10 minutes. Add milk and continue to simmer a few minutes.

Remove rind from Brie and cut into small pieces. Add to mixture along with red pepper. Stir until completely melted. Add oysters and scallions. Remove from heat; pour in champagne. Stir gently. Taste to correct seasonings. Cover and let stand 10 minutes before serving.

White Gazpacho

3   large cucumbers (about 2 pounds)
1½ cups seedless green grapes
1   medium avocado, chopped (about 1 cup)
1   large clove garlic, chopped
1   cup yogurt
1   cup sour cream
1   teaspoon salt or to taste
½   teaspoon ground white pepper
3   cups chicken broth
3   tablespoons dry vermouth

Garnish:
1½ cups halved seedless green grapes
1½ cups cubed avocado
1   cup chopped scallions, including green
     tops
1   cup chopped green bell pepper

Peel and seed cucumbers; cut into 2-inch pieces. Cut grapes in half. Peel and chop avocado. Combine with garlic in processor or blender; process a few seconds, leaving some texture in mixture. Pour into large bowl; add yogurt, sour cream, salt, pepper, chicken broth, and vermouth. Mix well; taste to adjust seasonings. Cover; chill overnight. Serve with bowls of garnishes.

Avocado and Pear Vinaigrette

SERVES 6

3   large ripe avocados
3   pears

Dressing:
2   tablespoons finely chopped green bell
    pepper
2   tablespoons finely chopped scallions
2   tablespoons finely chopped parsley
2   tablespoons raspberry vinegar
5   tablespoons walnut oil
⅛   teaspoon sugar
Salt and pepper to taste

Cut avocados in half; slice. Peel and core pears; slice. Divide pear and avocado slices among six individual serving dishes, arranging in attractive pattern. Spoon over 1 to 2 tablespoons of dressing. Chill slightly before serving.

To make dressing: Blanch green pepper and scallions 1 minute. Drain and refresh with cool water. Drain well; mix with other ingredients.

Mango Salad

SERVES 12

4   cups unsweetened pineapple juice
2   3-ounce packages lemon-flavored gelatin
2   large fresh ripe mangoes or 2 15-ounce
    cans mango, drained
2   8-ounce packages cream cheese
1   tablespoon lemon juice
Fresh mint sprigs for garnish

Heat pineapple juice and lemon-flavored gelatin until gelatin has dissolved. Set aside to cool.

Purée mangoes and mix well with cream cheese. Add lemon juice. Mix cheese into pineapple juice; pour into 10-cup mold. Chill until firm (about 4 to 6 hours). Unmold on serving platter and garnish with fresh mint sprigs.

Marinated Mushrooms

YIELDS I PINT

1 pound small mushrooms
1 quart water
1 teaspoon salt
1 teaspoon lemon juice

Marinade:
¾ cup mushroom liquid
¾ cup cider vinegar
2 large onions, sliced
2 tablespoons chopped parsley
1 teaspoon salt
2 teaspoons sugar
¼ teaspoon cracked pepper
1 clove garlic
1 bay leaf, crumbled

Preservative:
2 to 4 tablespoons olive oil

Wash mushrooms. Use sharp knife to remove all but ¼ inch of stems. Bring mushrooms, water, salt, and lemon juice to boil in enamel or stainless steel saucepan. Simmer, uncovered, 10 to 12 minutes, longer if mushrooms are large. Remove mushrooms from liquid with slotted spoon; reserve ¾ cup liquid.

Combine marinade ingredients in small saucepan. Bring to boil; simmer 10 minutes.

Place mushrooms in refrigerator container. Pour marinade over. Stir to distribute onion rings evenly among mushrooms. Gently pour thin stream of olive oil on top to keep air out. Chill overnight before serving. Use in salads or as mild savory.

Spinach Salad with Chicken Livers

SERVES 4 TO 6

2 10-ounce packages fresh spinach
8 to 10 whole chicken livers
2 tablespoons olive oil
Salt and pepper to taste
2 tablespoons wine vinegar

Dressing:
3 scallions, finely chopped
4 tablespoons finely chopped parsley
1 teaspoon chopped fresh chervil or ½ teaspoon dried chervil
1 teaspoon chopped fresh tarragon or ½ teaspoon dried tarragon
3 tablespoons wine vinegar
2 teaspoons Dijon mustard
6 tablespoons vegetable oil
Salt and pepper to taste

Wash spinach; remove stalks; dry leaves well. Wrap in towels. Refrigerate until ready to use.

Clean chicken livers, removing connective tissue.

Heat olive oil in skillet; sauté livers in very hot oil 1 to 2 minutes or until brown on outside but pink in center. Remove from skillet; slice and season with salt and pepper. Place on cold spinach leaves. Pour out any oil remaining in skillet; add vinegar. Bring to boil to deglaze pan. Pour vinegar over liver and spinach. Mix well and serve at once with dressing or vinaigrette (see p. 225).

To make dressing: Mix all ingredients together; shake until salt has dissolved.

Corn Relish

YIELDS 1¾ CUPS

⅓ cup sugar
1 tablespoon cornstarch
½ small onion, finely chopped (about ¼ cup)
1 teaspoon ground turmeric
½ teaspoon celery seed
¼ cup vinegar
¼ cup water
1 12-ounce can whole kernel corn, drained
2 tablespoons finely chopped green bell pepper
1 tablespoon chopped pimiento

In saucepan, combine sugar, cornstarch, onion, turmeric, celery seed, vinegar, water, and corn. Cook and stir until mixture thickens and bubbles. Stir in green pepper and pimiento. Chill.

Ratatouille Relish

YIELDS 6 CUPS

2 medium green bell peppers, stems and seeds removed
2 tomatoes, cored
1 medium onion
1 medium zucchini
½ small eggplant, peeled
2 tablespoons salt
1 cup sugar
1 cup vinegar
1 cup water
1 teaspoon mustard seed
¾ teaspoon celery seed
¼ teaspoon fines herbes

Chop by hand or use coarse blade of food chopper to chop peppers, tomatoes, onion, zucchini, and eggplant. Stir salt into vegetables; refrigerate overnight.

Rinse vegetables under cool water; drain.

In medium saucepan, combine sugar, vinegar, water, mustard seed, celery seed, and fines herbes. Stir in vegetables. Bring to boil; reduce heat and simmer 5 minutes, stirring frequently. Cool; cover. Chill until ready to use.

Basic Vegetable Preparations

To Blanch: For asparagus, broccoli, Brussels sprouts, carrots, cauliflower, green beans, and fresh peas.

Peel, trim, and cut vegetables to uniform-size pieces. Cut broccoli and cauliflower stems into smaller pieces than the florets or cut a deep cross in order to equalize cooking time. In large kettle bring salted water to boil. Drop in vegetable and boil. Approximate times:

asparagus: 5 to 10 minutes

broccoli: 3 to 5 minutes

Brussels sprouts and cauliflower: 10 to 15 minutes

green beans: 6 to 12 minutes

green peas and snow peas: 30 seconds

Times will vary according to size of pieces and freshness of vegetable. Test for doneness by biting into a piece. Drain immediately. Plunge vegetables into cold water to stop cooking and set color. To serve, heat vegetable in butter or oil; season with salt, herbs, citrus juice, and so on. Or dress with Béchamel sauce (see p. 224), hollandaise sauce (see p. 222), herb butter (see p. 222), or pesto (see p. 223).

To Steam: Prepare vegetable as above. Place on perforated steamer over small amount of boiling water or stock. Steaming time will vary. Check for doneness as above. Season as above.

To Quick Pot-Roast: Use only tender young vegetables. Prepare as above. Melt butter in skillet with tightly fitting lid. Add a little finely chopped onion or scallion, if desired. Distribute vegetable pieces over skillet and cover with dripping-wet lettuce leaf. Cover; cook very short time; length of cooking time will vary. Season with salt and pepper.

Cauliflower Polonaise

SERVES 6 TO 8

1 whole fresh cauliflower
6 tablespoons butter
½ cup bread crumbs
1 hard-boiled egg, finely chopped

Steam whole cauliflower until tender.

Melt butter in sauté pan and cook slowly until it turns golden (about 10 minutes). Add bread crumbs and continue to cook until mixture turns chocolate brown. Add chopped egg and mix well. Pour on top of whole cauliflower.

Chayote Sautée

SERVES 4 TO 6

3 medium-size chayotes
4 tablespoons butter
4 tablespoons water
¼ teaspoon salt
⅛ teaspoon freshly grated nutmeg

Wash chayotes; drop unpeeled into boiling water. Return to boil and cook 12 minutes. Drain and refresh under running cold water. Cut vegetables into quarters. Peel; remove seed. Cut each quarter into 3 slices lengthwise.

Melt butter in skillet large enough to hold slices in single layer. After putting chayote in pan, turn to coat with butter. Add water; cook over medium heat 5 minutes. Uncover; continue to cook, turning twice, until golden (about 5 minutes). Season with salt and nutmeg.

Eggplant alla Romano

3   medium eggplants
1½   pounds sweet Italian sausage (about 6
     sausages)
3   tablespoons vegetable oil
½   cup chopped onion
2   cloves garlic, finely chopped
1   16-ounce can peeled whole tomatoes
1   teaspoon dried oregano
1   teaspoon dried basil
1   teaspoon salt
⅛   teaspoon pepper
6   ounces grated provolone cheese (omit
     salt if imported)

Topping:
2   tablespoons butter
1   cup fine cracker crumbs
1½   teaspoons dried oregano

Preheat oven to 375°.

Cut eggplants in half lengthwise. Remove pulp, leaving ¼-inch border. Chop pulp.

Slip sausage from casing. Break up sausage; brown in heavy skillet. Remove sausage to paper towel to drain. Add vegetable oil to drippings; sauté onion, garlic, and chopped eggplant until soft. Add tomatoes, oregano, basil, salt, and pepper. Simmer until thick (about 15 minutes). Add cheese and mix well. Spoon into eggplant shells. Put shells in roasting pan with ½ inch water. Cover with aluminum foil, bake 20 minutes.

Melt butter and combine with cracker crumbs and oregano. Spoon over eggplant halves and bake, uncovered, additional 20 minutes.

Gratin of Eggplant

2   eggplants (about 2¼ pounds total
     weight)
1   teaspoon salt
Olive oil to brush slices

Tomato Sauce:
1½   tablespoons olive oil
2   cups finely chopped onion
3   cups tomatoes, peeled, seeded, and
     chopped (canned tomatoes, drained, may
     be substituted)
2   cloves garlic, finely chopped
1   teaspoon salt
4   drops Tabasco sauce

Cheese Sauce:
1   cup cottage cheese, drained
1   egg
¼   teaspoon freshly ground pepper
¾   cup grated Parmesan cheese, divided
½   cup heavy cream

To Finish Dish:
8 to 10 fresh basil leaves, torn into pieces
½   cup freshly grated Parmesan cheese
1   tablespoon finely chopped parsley

Preheat oven to 425°.

Slice unpeeled eggplant into ⅜-inch slices, sprinkle with salt, place in colander. Drain 30 minutes. Dry slices, place in single layer on baking sheet and brush well with olive oil. Broil until brown and slightly soft. Turn slices and repeat. Set aside.

To make tomato sauce: In heavy skillet, sauté onion in oil until soft. Add tomatoes, garlic, and seasonings. Cover. Simmer 5 minutes for tomato to render juices. Uncover. Raise heat, stir, and cook about 10 to 15 minutes until liquid has almost evaporated. Taste for salt.

To make cheese sauce: Mix cottage cheese and egg until smooth, using processor or blender. Add pepper and enough Parmesan cheese to make thick paste. Stir in cream until sauce is thick but pourable. Add salt if desired.

Line bottom of 8 × 13 × 2–inch gratin dish with half of eggplant slices. Sprinkle with pepper, basil leaf pieces, and part of Parmesan cheese. Spoon tomato sauce over top. Press remaining eggplant into sauce. Spoon cheese sauce over top. Sprinkle generously with Parmesan cheese.

Bake 10 minutes. Reduce heat to 375°; bake additional 15 to 20 minutes until gratin is puffed and golden brown.

Garnish with parsley.

Green Beans with Lemon Walnut Dressing

SERVES 6

⅓ cup walnut pieces
1 pound small, young, fresh green beans
⅜ teaspoon salt, divided
3 tablespoons walnut oil or sesame seed oil
⅓ cup sliced shallots or scallions
½ teaspoon ground cardamom
2 tablespoons chopped fresh basil leaves or 1½ teaspoons dried basil
1 tablespoon lemon juice
1 tablespoon grated lemon zest

Preheat oven to 300°.

Spread walnuts in shallow pan; bake 10 minutes. Set aside.

Wash beans; remove tips; cut in half crosswise. Sprinkle with ¼ teaspoon salt. Steam until beans are just tender. Refresh with cold water. Drain; set aside.

Heat oil over medium heat in large, heavy skillet. Add shallots or scallions; sauté until limp. Add beans, walnuts, cardamom, basil, lemon juice, and remaining salt. Cook until thoroughly heated, stirring constantly. Do not overcook beans. Sprinkle with lemon zest. Pour into heated serving bowl. Serve immediately.

Ratatouille

SERVES 8

1¼ pounds eggplant, cubed (about 4 cups)
Salt
4 medium zucchini, cubed (about 4 cups)
3 large red bell peppers
½ cup olive oil
2 large onions, chopped (about 2 cups)
4 large cloves garlic, finely chopped
6 ripe tomatoes, peeled, seeded, and quartered (about 4 cups)
2 bay leaves
2 tablespoons fresh thyme or 2 teaspoons dried thyme
2 teaspoons salt
¾ teaspoon ground black pepper
½ cup dry white wine or dry vermouth
⅓ cup chopped fresh basil or 2 teaspoons dried basil
2 tablespoons lemon juice

Peel eggplant; cut into eighths lengthwise, slicing ½ inch thick. Sprinkle with salt; drain in colander 30 minutes. Press out as much moisture as possible; dry on paper towels. Set aside.

Cut unpeeled zucchini into similar size pieces; add to eggplant.

Remove seeds and veins from red peppers; slice into thin julienne. Add to other vegetables. Set aside.

In heavy large saucepan, heat olive oil; sauté onions and garlic until translucent. Add eggplant, zucchini, peppers, tomatoes, bay leaves, thyme, salt, pepper, and wine. Cover; cook on low heat 20 minutes. Uncover and cook 30 minutes or until excess moisture has evaporated. Stir frequently to avoid scorching.

Remove bay leaves; add basil and lemon juice. Mix well and serve hot or at room temperature.

Baked Tomato Halves

SERVES 4 TO 8

4	underripe tomatoes
1	teaspoon salt
½	teaspoon pepper
¼	cup flour
3	tablespoons butter
2	tablespoons brown sugar

Preheat oven to 400°.

Cut tomatoes in half. Trim to make halves stand level. Season with salt and pepper. Dip in flour. Melt butter; brown halves. Place on cookie sheet. Sprinkle with brown sugar. Bake 15 minutes.

Vegetable Terrine

YIELDS 2 QUARTS

10	ounces dried white beans
10 to 12	small carrots, peeled
1	10-ounce package frozen spinach
1	10-ounce package frozen cauliflower
1	10-ounce package frozen asparagus
6	tablespoons tomato sauce
¼	cup chopped fresh basil or ½ teaspoon dried basil
1	clove garlic, pressed
4	tablespoons butter
4	tablespoons flour
1½	cups cream
½	teaspoon grated nutmeg
½	teaspoon salt
½	teaspoon ground white pepper
4	eggs, beaten
1	teaspoon lemon juice
⅛	teaspoon curry powder
1	tablespoon grated Parmesan cheese

Cook dried white beans according to package directions. Set aside.

Blanch other vegetables as follows: carrots, 7 minutes; spinach, 4 minutes; cauliflower, 3 minutes; asparagus, 3 to 4 minutes. Drain and set aside.

Simmer cooked beans with tomato sauce, basil, and garlic over low fire until liquid is almost evaporated.

Make Béchamel sauce as follows: melt butter in pan, stir in flour, and cook over low heat 2 minutes. Add cream, nutmeg, salt, and pepper. Cook until thickened, stirring constantly. Cool and add beaten eggs. Mix well.

Preheat oven to 350°.

Line 2-quart terrine with foil or waxed paper. Layer vegetables as follows: Blend spinach, ⅓ of Béchamel, and lemon juice together. Pour into terrine. Place cooked carrots lengthwise over spinach layer. Blend cauliflower with curry, ⅓ of Béchamel, and Parmesan. Spread evenly and carefully over carrots. Place asparagus lengthwise over cauliflower. Purée bean mixture with remaining Béchamel until smooth and pour over asparagus, smoothing carefully.

Place terrine in pan with ¾ inch hot water and bake 1 hour. Remove from oven; cool and chill overnight. Unmold and slice carefully in ½- to ¾-inch slices. Serve as first course with white wine or as luncheon entrée.

Baked Eggs Provençal

SERVES 4

4   tablespoons butter
2   shallots, finely chopped
1   tablespoon chopped fresh basil or 1 tea-
     spoon dried basil
½   tablespoon chopped fresh oregano or ½
     teaspoon dried oregano
2   tomatoes, peeled, seeded, and chopped
4   baked pastry shells (see pâté brisée,
     p. 254, or pastry for luncheon tart,
     p. 240)
4   large eggs
½   cup hollandaise sauce (see p. 222)

Preheat oven to 350°.
In butter, sauté shallots, basil, and oregano until tender. Add tomatoes; cook 2 minutes. Spoon mixture evenly into pastry shells. Break fresh egg in each pastry shell; bake 12 minutes. Remove from oven; top with hollandaise sauce.

Eggs Augustyn

SERVES 4

5   tablespoons butter
1   shallot, finely chopped
½   cup ham, cut into thin strips, divided
¾   cup fresh mushrooms
4   large tomatoes
4   large eggs
½   cup hollandaise sauce (see p. 222)

Preheat oven to 325°.
Sauté shallot in butter. Add ⅓ cup ham and mushrooms; cook 3 to 4 minutes. Purée mixture in blender or processor. Strain mixture to remove mushroom juice. Reserve juice.
Seed and scoop out centers of tomatoes. Fill tomatoes with mushroom mixture. Break egg in tomatoes; bake on cookie sheet 12 to 15 minutes.
Mix mushroom juice with hollandaise sauce. Spoon sauce over tomatoes and garnish with remaining ham.

Fail-Proof Frittata

5   tablespoons vegetable oil, divided
¾   cup chopped green bell pepper
1½ cups sliced fresh mushrooms
1½ cups coarsely chopped zucchini
¾   cup finely chopped onion
1   large clove garlic, pressed
6   eggs, beaten
¼   cup half-and-half
1   pound cream cheese, cubed
1½ cups grated Cheddar cheese
2   cups cubed bread
1   teaspoon salt
¼   teaspoon ground black pepper

Preheat oven to 325°.

Heat 3 tablespoons oil in heavy 10½-inch skillet. Sauté first five ingredients. Remove; set aside. Pour remaining 2 tablespoons oil in skillet. Set aside.

Mix eggs and half-and-half. Set aside.

Mix cheeses, bread, salt, and pepper; combine all three mixtures in large bowl. Pour into skillet or well-buttered 2-quart rectangular baking dish. Bake 30 minutes in skillet or 40 minutes in glass dish.

Note: May be assembled several hours or night before baking.

Blue Cheese Tarts

Crust:
1   3-ounce package cream cheese
8   tablespoons butter
1   cup flour

Filling:
2   large eggs
½   teaspoon salt
⅛   teaspoon ground white pepper
1   teaspoon onion juice
1   teaspoon flour
⅓   cup milk
5   ounces blue cheese

Preheat oven to 375°.

To make crust: Blend cream cheese and butter. Add flour to make dough. Form small balls. Place one in each cup of 2-inch muffin tin. Spread dough with fingers to line cup. Set aside. Chill.

To make filling: Beat eggs. Add salt, pepper, onion juice, and flour. Stir well. Blend milk into cheese. Stir into egg mixture. Spoon 2 teaspoons of filling into each pastry cup. Bake 15 to 20 minutes or until well browned. Serve warm.

Chile Quiche

SERVES 4 TO 6

2 3-ounce cans whole green chilies,
   drained
1¼ cups grated sharp Cheddar cheese
1¼ cups grated Swiss cheese
5 eggs, beaten
½ teaspoon salt
¼ teaspoon Tabasco sauce
1¼ teaspoons Worcestershire sauce

Preheat oven to 300°.
Line 9-inch greased pie pan with chilies.
Mix cheeses; place in pan. Add seasonings
to beaten eggs; pour over cheese. Bake
40 minutes.

Variation: Mushrooms, ham, onions, or
chicken may be added.

Cold Tomato-Cheese Luncheon Tart

SERVES 6 TO 8

Filling:
⅓ cup sour cream
2 tablespoons finely chopped green bell
   pepper
1 teaspoon finely chopped onion
1¼ teaspoons salt
⅛ teaspoon ground white pepper
½ pound Swiss cheese, cubed
¼ cup crumbled blue cheese
½ cup whipping cream
2 cups fresh tomatoes, skinned, cubed, and
   drained

Crust:
1½ cups flour
½ teaspoon salt
¼ teaspoon dry mustard
6 tablespoons butter
1 cup shredded Cheddar cheese
1 egg yolk
1 to 2 tablespoons water

Garnish (optional):
Thin slices of tomatoes
2 tablespoons finely chopped parsley

To make filling: Blend all filling ingredients except cream and tomatoes. Chill
several hours.

To make crust: Sift together flour, salt,
and mustard. Cut in butter until mixture is
size of small peas. Add cheese.
Combine egg yolk with water; stir into
flour mixture with fork until it forms a ball.
Roll out and fit into 9-inch pie pan. Prick
sides and bottom; chill 1 hour.
Preheat oven to 400°.
Bake 20 minutes; cool.

When ready to serve: Whip cream. Fold
cream and tomatoes into chilled filling mixture; pour into pastry shell. Garnish with
slices of tomato and parsley if desired.
Good served with cold, marinated shrimp,
crab legs, or lobster.

Dilly Cheese Custards

SERVES 6

2	3-ounce packages pimiento cream cheese
¼	cup white wine
½	cup cream
1	teaspoon seasoned salt
½	teaspoon dry mustard
½	teaspoon dried dill weed
1	tablespoon finely chopped green onion
1	tablespoon finely chopped pimiento
4	eggs

Parsley for garnish

Preheat oven to 375°.

Soften cheese; beat in wine and cream until smooth. Stir in salt, mustard, dill, onion, and pimiento.

Beat eggs and stir into cheese mixture, stirring until smooth.

Lightly butter bottoms of 6 3- to 4-ounce ramekins or custard cups. Pour in cheese custard and set cups in shallow pan with ½ inch hot water in bottom. Bake 25 minutes or until custards are set in center. Remove from water and let stand 5 minutes before turning out or serving in baking dishes. Garnish with parsley.

Baked Rice with Cheese

SERVES 6

4	eggs
2	cups cooked rice (½ cup long-grain rice uncooked)
1	teaspoon salt
¼	teaspoon dry mustard
¼	teaspoon paprika
1	cup cubed or grated sharp Cheddar cheese
1	tablespoon butter
1½	cups milk

Preheat oven to 325°.

Beat eggs lightly; add cooked rice, salt, mustard, and paprika.

Melt cheese and butter in milk in double boiler over hot water. Pour mixture over rice. Mix well. Place in 1-quart buttered casserole. Bake 1 hour or until knife inserted in center comes out clean.

Florentine Lasagna

SERVES 6

1¼	pounds ground beef
1	medium onion, finely chopped (about ½ cup)
1	clove garlic, finely chopped
1	3-ounce can sliced mushrooms with liquid
1	15-ounce can tomato sauce
1	6-ounce can tomato paste
2	teaspoons salt
1	teaspoon dried oregano
8	ounces lasagna noodles
1	egg, beaten
1	10-ounce package chopped spinach, thawed and drained
1	tablespoon oil
1	cup cottage cheese
⅓	cup grated Parmesan cheese
1½	cups grated mozzarella cheese

Preheat oven to 350°.

In skillet lightly brown ground beef. Add onion and garlic; stir until beef is completely browned and vegetables are translucent. Add mushrooms with liquid, tomato sauce, tomato paste, salt, and oregano. Simmer 15 minutes.

Cook lasagna noodles according to directions on package and drain. Mix well with beaten egg.

Mix spinach with oil, cottage cheese, and Parmesan cheese.

Pour half of meat mixture into 2½-quart oven-proof dish. Layer half of noodles over meat; spread entire spinach mixture onto noodles. Layer with remaining noodles and top with rest of meat mixture. Cover with foil; bake 45 minutes. Uncover. Arrange mozzarella cheese on top; return to oven for 10 minutes until cheese has melted.

Pasta with Mediterranean Sauce

SERVES 12 AS FIRST COURSE
OR 6 AS ENTRÉE

3   pounds fresh spinach
9   tablespoons butter
2   cloves garlic, finely chopped
2   tablespoons finely chopped anchovies *
⅔   cup finely chopped pine nuts
¾   teaspoon grated orange zest
Freshly ground pepper to taste
¼   teaspoon grated nutmeg to taste
1½   cups heavy cream
1½   cups grated Parmesan cheese, divided
1½   pounds pasta

Blanch spinach 1 minute in boiling, salted water. Drain; press to extract excess moisture. Chop finely. Put in 6-quart serving bowl and keep warm.

Heat butter in 10-inch skillet. Add garlic, anchovies, nuts, orange zest, pepper, and nutmeg. Stir and cook 2 minutes. Add cream. Stir well. Cook until heated thoroughly. Pour sauce over spinach. Add ¾ cup cheese; mix well.

Cook pasta "al dente" (not too soft); drain. Pour into bowl with sauce. With two forks, lift and turn pasta to coat with sauce. Serve immediately. Pass remaining cheese in separate bowl.

Note: If a heartier dish is desired, add 1 7½-ounce can imported snails, drained, to butter. Sauté with garlic, anchovies, nuts, and zest.

* No substitutes. Remove anchovies from tin; rinse under warm water; press dry between paper towels; then chop finely.

Pasta with Scallops and Parsley

SERVES 4 AS ENTRÉE
OR 6 TO 8 AS FIRST COURSE

4   tablespoons butter
2   shallots, finely chopped
⅔   cup finely chopped parsley, divided
½   cup dry white wine
1   pound scallops, cut across grain into ¼-inch slices
½   cup half-and-half
½   cup whipping cream
1   cup grated Parmesan cheese
¼ to ½ teaspoon grated nutmeg or to taste
½   teaspoon salt
⅛   teaspoon ground white pepper
16   ounces green and white linguine or fettuccine

Melt butter in 9-inch skillet. Sauté shallots and ¼ cup parsley 5 minutes, stirring constantly. Add wine and reduce to 6 tablespoonfuls. Add scallops and cook 1 minute. Add half-and-half and whipping cream. Stir once or twice. Remove from heat. Stir in Parmesan, ⅓ cup parsley, nutmeg, salt, and pepper. Set aside in warm place.

Prepare pasta according to directions, being careful not to overcook. Drain. Place in warm bowl.

Spoon scallops out of sauce into container. Toss pasta with sauce. Put pasta in serving dish or on plates; spoon scallops over pasta. Sprinkle with remaining parsley. Serve immediately.

SEAFOOD, POULTRY, AND MEAT

Poached Scallops with Raspberry Dressing   244

Curried Shrimp (Chicken, Lamb) with Almond Rice   244

Smoked Fish   245

Trout Vincent   245

Chinese Tuna Salad   246

Braised Chicken in Wine   246

Duck à la Bourbon   247

French Country Chicken   247

Amaretto Game Hens and Wild Rice   248

Braised Beef with Brandy   248

Roulades of Beef   249

Ham Loaf with Orange Sauce and Bananas   250

Rabbit for Two   250

Poached Scallops with Raspberry Dressing

SERVES 4

3   cups water
1   cup dry white wine
1   tablespoon salt
½   teaspoon ground white pepper
1   pound bay scallops

Dressing:
1   sliver garlic (about the size of an almond sliver)
¼   cup olive oil
¼   cup vegetable oil
½   cup raspberry vinegar
½   teaspoon salt
⅛   teaspoon ground white pepper
1   tablespoon crème fraîche (see p. 222)
½   teaspoon dried tarragon or more to taste
Avocados, cherry tomatoes, bibb or red tip lettuce, and purple onion for garnish (optional)

Bring water, wine, salt, and pepper to simmer. Add scallops; cook 2 to 3 minutes over low heat. Remove from heat. Cover; allow to remain in liquid 5 minutes. Drain. Do not overcook or scallops will be tough.

Mix remaining ingredients except tarragon; process until smooth. Add tarragon and process briefly. Serve scallops on lettuce with dressing. Garnish with avocado slices, cherry tomatoes, and slices of purple onion if desired.

Curried Shrimp (Chicken, Lamb) with Almond Rice

SERVES 6

Almond Rice:
1   cup long-grain rice
2   cups water
1   teaspoon salt
1   teaspoon vinegar
3   tablespoons butter, divided
¼ to ½ cup slivered almonds

Curry:
4   tablespoons vegetable oil
2   large onions, sliced paper thin (about 2 cups)
1   tart apple, peeled, cored, quartered, and sliced paper thin (about 1 cup)
2   cloves garlic, pressed
1   teaspoon finely chopped fresh gingerroot or ½ teaspoon ground ginger or to taste
1   tablespoon curry powder or to taste
4   tablespoons flour
½   teaspoon salt
½   teaspoon freshly ground pepper
3   cups strong chicken broth (see p. 221)
2   pounds cooked shrimp (see p. 100)
Condiments (all or any of the following): chutney (this is essential; see pp. 22 and 54), grated coconut, chopped bacon, chopped egg, sliced bananas (sautéed in butter), chopped cucumber, yogurt, chopped tomatoes, chopped scallions

Put rice, water, salt, vinegar, and 1 tablespoon butter in 2-quart saucepan with tight-fitting lid. Cover; bring to boil over high heat. As soon as rice boils, reduce to lowest heat. Cover; cook 30 minutes.

Cook onions, apple, garlic, and ginger in oil in 2-quart heavy saucepan until onion is lightly browned. Add curry powder, flour, salt, and pepper, stirring until well blended. Gradually add broth, stirring constantly. Cook until slightly thickened. Add shrimp; simmer until thoroughly heated. Do not overcook or shrimp will be tough.

Melt remaining butter; sauté almonds until lightly browned. Set aside. When rice is done, toss almonds and rice with two forks. Put rice and curry in separate serving bowls, surrounded by condiments.

Smoked Fish

1   domed charcoal smoker
5   pounds charcoal
1   chunk mesquite, hickory, or pecan (approximately 4 × 4 × 2½ inches)
Full pan of water

Set up smoker, placing charcoal in bottom of charcoal pan according to manufacturer's directions. Add small amount charcoal lighter fluid in center. Light; when flames die down, place mesquite in center. Place water pan over charcoal container. Seasonings, such as herbs, lemon slices, or tea leaves, may be added to water. Place grill over pan of water. Put fish on grill. Cover with domed lid; allow fish to smoke 1 to 3 hours, depending on desired texture. Add more liquid as necessary.

To smoke whole fish: Cover fish liberally with vegetable oil. Salt lightly inside and out. Oil grill well to prevent sticking. Smoke as above, allowing 1 to 1½ hours for 1-pound fish or 2 to 2½ hours for 3-pound fish.

To smoke fish chunks: Skin fish; cut into 2½-inch chunks. Place in disposable foil pan approximately 11 × 13 × 3 inches. Smoke as above.

Note: Speckled trout, redfish, red snapper, salmon, kingfish, freshwater trout, bass, and other varieties are suited to smoking.

Trout Vincent

SERVES 6

2   quarts court bouillon (see p. 220)
3   small fresh-water trout, cleaned and scaled

Sauce:
¼   cup low-fat cottage cheese
½   cup mayonnaise (see p. 223)
1   teaspoon Dijon mustard or to taste
1   teaspoon fresh lime juice or to taste
½   teaspoon finely chopped fresh garlic, chives, or tarragon
1   tablespoon finely chopped parsley

Garnish:
2   heads Boston lettuce, broken into pieces or separated into leaves
2   lemons, sliced
12   sprigs parsley

In 4-quart stainless steel or enamel saucepan, bring court bouillon to boil. Reduce heat to simmer. Add trout; cook approximately 3 minutes, uncovered. Remove pot from heat. Cool trout in liquid 45 minutes. Remove trout to cutting board. Pull off skin, beginning at tail and moving toward head. Remove head and tail. Filet trout, removing all bones. Wrap filets individually in plastic wrap. Refrigerate until ready to serve.

Purée cottage cheese in blender until smooth. Remove to bowl; stir in remaining ingredients. Refrigerate 1 to 2 hours. Serve on bed of lettuce; garnish with lemon slices and parsley. Spoon small amount of sauce on trout; pass remainder in sauceboat.

Chinese Tuna Salad

2   6½-ounce cans white albacore tuna, water packed (no substitutes)
1   10-ounce package frozen peas, thawed and drained
2   ribs celery, finely chopped (about 1 cup)
1   8-ounce can sliced water chestnuts, drained
1   tablespoon lemon juice
1   tablespoon soy sauce
½   teaspoon curry powder
1   cup mayonnaise (see p. 223)
1   3-ounce can Chinese noodles
1   2½-ounce package slivered toasted almonds

Drain tuna and break into chunks. Add peas, celery, and water chestnuts. Mix lemon juice, soy sauce, and curry powder with mayonnaise. Toss lightly with tuna mixture. Chill well. Just before serving mix in noodles and almonds.

Braised Chicken in Wine

3   tablespoons butter
¼   pound salt pork, chopped
1   medium onion, chopped (about ¾ cup)
2   carrots, sliced 1 inch thick
3   shallots, sliced
2   cloves garlic, finely chopped
1   chicken (2½ to 3 pounds), cut into pieces
3   tablespoons flour
2   tablespoons chopped parsley
1   tablespoon dried marjoram
½   bay leaf
½   teaspoon salt
½   teaspoon freshly ground pepper
2   cups dry sherry or white wine
½   pound mushrooms, sliced

In skillet melt butter. Add salt pork, onion, carrot, shallots, and garlic, stirring until lightly browned. Remove with slotted spoon; set aside.

In same skillet, brown chicken pieces. Set aside with vegetables.

To juices in pan, add flour, parsley, marjoram, bay leaf, salt, and pepper. Stir over low heat to make roux. Gradually add sherry, stirring until sauce is smooth and thickened. Place chicken and vegetables back into skillet. Simmer about 1 hour, turning pieces occasionally. Five minutes before serving, add mushrooms.

Duck à la Bourbon

SERVES 4

1   duckling (4½ pounds)
1   teaspoon salt
1   orange, quartered
1   clove garlic
¼   cup plus 2 tablespoons bourbon, divided
¼   cup melted butter
½   cup orange marmalade

Bourbon Sauce (yields about 1½ cups):
1½ tablespoons butter
1   duck liver
½   small clove garlic, finely chopped
3   tablespoons flour
⅛   teaspoon finely ground black pepper or
     to taste
½   teaspoon catsup
½   cup orange juice
½   cup chicken broth (see p. 221)
¼   cup red wine
2   tablespoons orange marmalade
¼   cup bourbon
1   tablespoon grated orange zest

Preheat oven to 450°.

Rinse duckling and pat dry. Fill duckling cavity with salt, orange quarters, garlic clove, and ¼ cup bourbon. Close cavity.

Place duckling on its back on rack in shallow roasting pan. Brush with butter. Roast uncovered 30 minutes. Reduce heat to 375°. Roast duckling 40 minutes, basting often with drippings. Turn duckling onto breast; roast 20 minutes, basting often. Turn duckling onto back; roast 30 minutes, basting often.

Combine marmalade and 2 tablespoons bourbon. Spread mixture on duckling breast and roast 10 additional minutes. Remove to warmed platter. Serve with bourbon sauce.

To make bourbon sauce: Melt butter in saucepan. Add duck liver and garlic. Cook over low heat until liver is browned on all sides. Remove liver and chop finely. Reserve drippings.

Add flour, pepper, and catsup to drippings. Blend well. Gradually add orange juice, broth, wine, marmalade, bourbon, and orange zest. Cook over low heat, stirring continuously until thickened. Add liver and cook additional 5 minutes.

French Country Chicken

SERVES 4 TO 6

4   whole chicken breasts, split and boned
1   teaspoon salt
½   teaspoon ground white pepper
¼   cup olive oil
2   medium onions, sliced (about 1½ cups)
1   red bell pepper, cut into 1-inch pieces
     (about ½ cup)
1   green bell pepper, cut into 1-inch pieces
     (about ½ cup)
4   zucchini, sliced (about 3 cups)
2   14½-ounce cans whole peeled tomatoes,
     drained
8   ounces fresh mushrooms, cut in half
     (about 1½ cups)
3   cloves garlic, pressed
2   tablespoons finely chopped parsley
2   teaspoons fresh basil or ½ teaspoon
     dried basil
1   teaspoon fresh thyme or ½ teaspoon
     dried thyme
3   teaspoons fresh tarragon or 2 teaspoons
     dried tarragon

Season chicken breasts with salt and pepper. Brown in olive oil in large Dutch oven. Remove chicken.

Add onion and pepper; sauté 5 minutes. Add rest of ingredients. Cover; simmer 20 minutes. Add chicken. Cook additional 15 minutes or until chicken is done. Adjust seasonings. Serve over rice or in large soup plates with crusty French bread.

Amaretto Game Hens and Wild Rice

SERVES 4

¾ cup brown rice
¾ cup wild rice
1 large rib celery, chopped (about ⅔ cup)
1 cup sliced mushrooms
⅓ cup finely chopped scallions
2 tablespoons chopped parsley
1 teaspoon salt
½ teaspoon paprika
1½ tablespoons ground black pepper
3½ cups chicken stock (see p. 221)
4 game hens
4 tablespoons Amaretto
2 tablespoons sliced almonds

Preheat oven to 350°.
In large covered roaster, place rice, celery, mushrooms, scallions, parsley, salt, paprika, and pepper. Add chicken stock; stir. Place game hens on top of rice mixture. Cover. Bake 1 hour and 15 minutes.
Mix Amaretto and almonds. Remove lid from roasting pan; raise temperature to 425°. Baste hens with almond mixture. Continue to cook about 15 minutes or until brown. Arrange birds on top of bed of rice on platter.

Braised Beef with Brandy

SERVES 6 TO 8

2 pounds sirloin tip, cut into 2-inch pieces
1 teaspoon garlic salt
1 teaspoon paprika
½ teaspoon dried basil
¼ teaspoon dried thyme
2 tablespoons flour
2 tablespoons oil
1 large onion, cut into wedges
½ cup brandy
1 10½-ounce can beef broth
2 cups sliced fresh mushrooms
1 tablespoon butter
3 to 4 fresh carrots, sliced
¼ pound fresh green beans, cut into bite-size lengths
Chopped parsley for garnish

Preheat oven to 350°.
Mix meat with garlic salt, paprika, basil, thyme, and flour until well covered.
Heat oil in heavy pan and brown meat. Transfer meat to 3-quart oven-proof casserole dish.
Sauté onion in remaining oil; add to casserole.
Deglaze pan with brandy. Add broth. Simmer 10 minutes. Pour liquid over meat in casserole. Cover; bake 1 hour or until meat is tender.
While meat is cooking, sauté mushrooms in 1 tablespoon butter. Set aside. Drain off accumulated juices.
Blanch carrots and beans separately in boiling water. Drain; run each under cold water. Drain and set aside.
When meat is tender, add vegetables. Cook 15 additional minutes. Sprinkle with chopped parsley before serving.

Roulades of Beef

SERVES 6

2   pounds beef (sirloin tip in one piece)

Marinade:
1   bottle dry red wine
1   onion, sliced (about ⅔ cup)
1   small carrot, sliced (about ½ cup)
2   tablespoons oil
2   tablespoons red wine vinegar
12 peppercorns
2   tablespoons butter
1   teaspoon oil

Stuffing:
2   cloves garlic, finely chopped
4   ounces very lean slab bacon, cut into small pieces
4   large shallots, finely chopped
¼ cup finely chopped parsley
Freshly ground black pepper

Sauce:
2   tablespoons butter
2   tablespoons flour
1½ cups beef broth or stock (see p. 220), heated to boiling
1   tablespoon tomato paste
Bouquet garni: parsley, bayleaf, and thyme tied up in cheesecloth or garni bag
Salt to taste

Slice meat thinly; cut into small squares (approximately 3 × 3 inches).

To prepare marinade: Mix all ingredients together. Place slices of meat in large oven-proof or glazed earthenware dish; add marinade and cover with wax paper. Refrigerate 6 hours or overnight. Turn meat several times.

Prepare stuffing by mixing ingredients in small bowl.

To prepare brown sauce: Melt butter over low heat. Blend in flour and cook slowly, stirring until butter and flour froth together 2 minutes without coloring. Remove roux from heat; pour in hot broth all at once. Beat vigorously with wire whisk to blend. Cook over moderate heat, stirring; add tomato paste and bouquet garni. Taste for salt.

Remove meat from marinade and set aside. Cook reserved marinade ½ hour, reducing it to approximately 2 cups. Strain and mix into brown sauce.

Dry meat with paper towel. Place 1 teaspoon stuffing on each piece. Roll meat using toothpick to hold roll together.

Heat butter and oil in large skillet. Sear roulades on all sides. Allow meat to simmer in own juice 10 minutes. Strain grease from pan. Cover with brown sauce. Season lightly with salt and generously with pepper. Cook on low heat 40 to 50 minutes. Remove bouquet garni before serving.

Ham Loaf with Orange Sauce and Bananas

SERVES 8

Ham Loaf:
1	pound ham, ground
½	pound fresh pork, ground
½	pound round steak, ground
¼	cup chopped onion
½	cup wheat germ
2	eggs
1	cup cracker crumbs
¾	cup milk
1	teaspoon salt (taste ham for salt and adjust amount if necessary)

Orange Sauce:
⅓	cup brown sugar
1	tablespoon cornstarch
¼	teaspoon ground cloves
½	cup orange juice
2	tablespoons honey
2	tablespoons rum

Garnish:
4	bananas
Parsley sprigs	

Preheat oven to 400°.

To make loaf: Mix all ingredients together; place in 9 × 5–inch loaf pan. Bake 1½ hours, basting occasionally with orange sauce.

To make sauce: Combine brown sugar, cornstarch, and cloves in small saucepan. Stir in orange juice, honey, and rum. Cook until mixture thickens, stirring constantly.

To prepare bananas: Peel and halve lengthwise; place in shallow baking dish. Add remaining sauce and bake in oven along with loaf last 10 minutes. Garnish with parsley sprigs.

Rabbit for Two

SERVES 2

4	slices bacon, finely chopped
2-pound cottontail rabbit * (cut into serving pieces)	
½	teaspoon salt
¼	teaspoon green peppercorns (crushed)
¼	cup flour
1	large onion, finely chopped (about 1 cup)
2	cloves garlic, finely chopped
¾	cup dry red wine
¾	cup chicken stock (see p. 221)
¼	teaspoon dried thyme
¼	teaspoon dried rosemary
1	bay leaf

In large heavy casserole, fry bacon until crisp. Drain and set aside.

Wash rabbit, pat dry, salt and pepper and lightly dust with flour. Over high heat, brown rabbit in bacon fat. Transfer pieces to plate.

Sauté onions and garlic in remaining bacon drippings 4 minutes. Add wine, stock, and herbs; return rabbit to pot. Add bacon pieces; cover and simmer over low heat 2 to 3 hours or until rabbit is tender. During last 30 minutes of cooking, extra stock may be needed. Correct seasonings.

* Domestic rabbit may be substituted.

BREADS, DESSERTS, AND CANDIES

Foundation Recipe for Fritters

SERVES 4

2   eggs
⅔   cup milk
½   teaspoon salt
1   tablespoon melted butter
1   cup flour
1   teaspoon baking powder
Vegetable oil

Beat eggs and milk until smooth. Add salt and melted butter, mixing thoroughly.

Sift together flour and baking powder. Add to egg. Beat until smooth.

Heat 2 inches of vegetable oil in skillet to 375°. Drop mixture by teaspoonfuls into oil. Fry 3 to 5 minutes or until crisp and brown. Remove fritters to paper towels to drain. Serve immediately.

Variations: Rice fritters: Add 1 tablespoon sugar and 1 cup cooked rice to fritter mixture.

Corn fritters: Add 1 7-ounce can whole kernel corn, drained.

Fruit fritters: Add 2 to 4 tablespoons sugar, 1 cup sliced or chopped fruit (apples, pears, or bananas), and 1 teaspoon cinnamon or ½ teaspoon nutmeg (optional).

Jewish Rye Bread

YIELDS 3 LOAVES

3   cups warm water (110°)
2   packages or 2 scant tablespoons active dry yeast
1   tablespoon sugar
2   tablespoons shortening
2   tablespoons salt
3   cups rye flour
5 to 9 cups bread flour, divided
2   tablespoons caraway seeds
1   egg white beaten with 1 tablespoon water for glaze
Additional caraway seeds for top

Pour warm water into large mixing bowl. Sprinkle yeast and sugar over water; let set 5 minutes. Add shortening, salt, rye flour, and 3 cups bread flour. Knead on low speed until well mixed. Add caraway seeds and enough remaining flour to make medium dough. (The amount may vary a great deal, depending on the humidity and preference as to feel of dough.) It should be soft but not sticky. Knead 10 minutes on low speed in mixer with dough hook or knead by hand, actively, 20 minutes. Cover with towel or plastic wrap. Place in warm, draft-free area; let rise until doubled.

Separate into 3 loaf portions. Shape into wide oval loaves. Place on baking sheet. Glaze with egg white and water mixture. Sprinkle generously with caraway seeds. Let rise until almost double in size. Score closely, about ½ inch apart straight across loaves and about ½ inch deep.

Preheat oven to 400°.

Bake 10 minutes, using pan of hot water in oven for steam. Remove water. Continue baking 30 to 40 minutes or until loaves sound hollow when tapped.

Orange Crumb French Toast

SERVES 4

2 eggs
¼ teaspoon salt
⅔ cup orange juice
1½ cups fine dry bread crumbs
1 teaspoon grated orange zest
8 slices white bread
1 tablespoon shortening
2 tablespoons butter

Syrup:
1 cup maple syrup
¼ cup orange juice
1 teaspoon grated orange zest

Combine eggs, salt, and orange juice; beat together thoroughly.

Combine bread crumbs with orange zest. Dip bread slices in orange-egg mixture, then in the crumb mixture, turning slices to coat evenly.

Melt shortening and butter; brown bread on both sides on hot griddle.

Meanwhile combine ingredients for syrup; simmer 5 minutes. Serve French toast with hot orange syrup and butter.

Variation: Use whole wheat or raisin bread.

Sopapillas

YIELDS 3 DOZEN

1 package active dry yeast
½ cup warm water (110°)
1 teaspoon sugar
3 cups flour
1 tablespoon melted butter, cooled
1 teaspoon salt
1 egg
Oil for frying

Dissolve yeast in warm water with sugar.

Mix flour, butter, salt, and egg. Pour into yeast mixture. Add enough water to make firm, springy breadlike dough.

Knead 15 minutes. Cover with towel or plastic wrap. Place in warm, draft-free area; let rise 30 minutes or longer until doubled in bulk.

Punch down dough. Roll half of dough to ¼-inch thickness on lightly floured board. Cut into 2-inch squares.

Heat oil to 375°. Stretch squares gently and drop into hot oil. Hold down in oil until dough begins to puff; then turn squares over. Fry only three or four at a time and turn often until golden. Drain on absorbent paper. Repeat with remaining dough. Serve hot with butter and lots of honey.

Meringue Shell

YIELDS 8- OR 10-INCH RING OR ABOUT 8
2½- TO 3-INCH SHELLS

4   egg whites
¼   teaspoon cream of tartar
¼   teaspoon salt
1   teaspoon lemon juice
1   teaspoon vanilla extract (see p. 224)
1½ cups sugar

Preheat oven to 275°.

Beat egg whites with cream of tartar and salt until soft peaks form.

Combine lemon juice and vanilla extract.

Slowly add sugar to egg whites alternately with drops of the liquid while continuing to beat. Beat until sugar is dissolved and egg whites are very stiff.

Lightly grease 8-inch spring-form pan with vegetable oil. Place meringue in pan, smoothing around rim of pan. Bake 1 hour or until pale gold and crisp to touch. Turn off heat and leave meringue in oven until cooled. Remove from pan and place on serving dish.

When ready to serve, fill meringue with lightly sugared fresh fruit and whipped cream or slightly softened ice cream. Meringue can also be heaped in 10-inch pie plate and shaped with spatula into free-standing shell with heavy edge.

Pâté Brisée

YIELDS 1 9-INCH PASTRY SHELL
OR ABOUT 10 2-INCH TARTLETS

1½ cups flour
½   teaspoon salt
6   tablespoons cold butter cut into small pieces
3   tablespoons solid vegetable shortening
3   tablespoons ice water

Place flour, salt, butter, and shortening in chilled bowl. Blend rapidly until shortening resembles oatmeal flakes. Add ice water a tablespoon at a time, mixing well to form ball. If necessary add more water by the teaspoon. Wrap dough in wax paper. Refrigerate 30 minutes.

Roll out quickly between 2 sheets of wax paper and fit into 9-inch pie or tart pan.

To bake "blind" (empty): Prick bottom of crust all over with fork. Refrigerate 1 hour.

Preheat oven to 425°.

Fit foil into crust. Fill with dried beans. Bake 8 minutes. Remove beans and foil. Continue baking another 4 to 5 minutes. Cool and fill with precooked filling.

To bake with filling: Preheat oven to 425°.

Prebake crust 3 to 4 minutes to seal. Cool, fill, and continue baking according to recipe directions.

Banana Chocolate Chiffon Pie

SERVES 8

Crust:
1½ cups chocolate wafer crumbs
½   cup finely chopped almonds
½   cup powdered sugar
¼   pound butter, melted

Filling:
1   envelope unflavored gelatin
¾   cup unsweetened pineapple juice
3   eggs, separated
½   cup brown sugar, packed
3   bananas
¼   cup rum
¼   teaspoon salt
¼   teaspoon grated nutmeg
1   cup whipping cream
1   cup grated semisweet chocolate

Preheat oven to 300°.
Combine ingredients for crust and press into 10-inch pie plate. Sprinkle with cold water. Bake 8 minutes.

To make filling: Soften gelatin in pineapple juice. Set aside.
Beat egg yolks; add brown sugar; beat well.
Heat gelatin mixture. Stir in egg mixture. Cook over low heat just until sugar and gelatin have dissolved; stir constantly. Do not boil. Remove from heat and cool.
Purée bananas; add rum, salt, and nutmeg. Stir into mixture. Cool until it begins to thicken.
Beat egg whites until soft peaks form; fold into mixture. Beat whipping cream; fold into mixture. Pour into prepared crust. Sprinkle chocolate over top. Chill 4 to 6 hours.

Cranberry Velvet Pie

SERVES 6 TO 8

Crust:
1½ cups butter-flavored cookie crumbs
¼   pound butter, melted
½   cup chopped pecans
¼   cup powdered sugar

Filling:
5   tablespoons butter, softened
½   cup powdered sugar
2   eggs
8   ounces cream cheese, softened
1   cup cranberry-orange relish
1   cup whole cranberry sauce
2   tablespoons undiluted frozen orange juice
1   cup whipping cream

Preheat oven to 300°.
Mix ingredients for crust and press into 9-inch pie plate. Bake 8 minutes.

To make filling: Cream butter and sugar well. Add eggs one at a time; beat well after each addition. Add cream cheese; mix well. Add cranberry-orange relish, cranberry sauce, and orange juice.
Whip cream and fold in. Pour into prepared crust. Freeze 8 hours. Remove from freezer. Place in refrigerator 30 minutes before serving.

Date Pudding

SERVES 2 TO 4

2 egg whites
½ cup sugar
⅛ teaspoon salt
4 tablespoons flour
1 tablespoon baking powder
½ cup chopped nuts
½ cup chopped dates

Preheat oven to 350°.

Beat egg whites until stiff.

Sift together sugar, salt, flour, and baking powder. Fold egg whites into dry ingredients. Add dates and nuts.

Spoon batter into greased shallow 1-quart casserole. Place in shallow pan of water. Bake 30 minutes. Allow pudding to remain in oven for several minutes after fire is turned off. Serve warm or cool with whipped cream.

Mocha Dacquoise

SERVES 10 TO 12

Meringues:
⅔ cup sugar
1 tablespoon cornstarch
1 cup ground blanched almonds
½ teaspoon salt
5 egg whites
Powdered sugar for garnish

Buttercream:
⅓ cup sugar
¼ cup cold water
5 egg yolks
½ pound butter, softened
1 tablespoon instant coffee, preferably espresso
1½ ounces semisweet chocolate, melted
1 ounce unsweetened chocolate, melted

Rum Cream Filling:
½ cup whipping cream
1 tablespoon dark Jamaica rum
1 teaspoon sugar

Preheat oven to 350°.

Butter and flour 2 baking sheets, shaking off excess flour. Draw 2 9-inch circles on prepared sheets. Set aside.

To make meringues: Combine sugar, cornstarch, and ground almonds in small bowl.

Beat salt and egg whites until stiff but not dry. Gently fold in sugar-nut mixture with rubber spatula, working as rapidly as possible. Spread mixture evenly on circles and smooth with spatula. Bake in center of oven about 20 minutes, checking after 15 minutes. If meringues brown too rapidly, lower heat. When done, meringues should be golden brown and crisp. Remove from oven; cool on racks.

To make buttercream: Bring sugar and water to boiling point; boil 2 minutes or until mixture threads (230° to 232°). Remove from heat. In electric mixer beat egg yolks. With mixer running pour hot syrup over yolks. Continue to beat at high speed 4 to 5 minutes until mixture thickens and cools to lukewarm. Lower speed to medium. Add butter, one small piece at a time. Beat until mixture is smooth. Stir in coffee powder and melted chocolate. Place in refrigerator a few minutes until firm enough to handle.

For top layer: Trim edges of one meringue as necessary to make perfect circle. Save trimmings. Lightly sprinkle meringue with powdered sugar.

Fill pastry sleeve with buttercream and, using star tip, decorate edge of meringue with fluted piping. Pipe a rosette in center. Set aside.

Pipe similar edge on other meringue. Spread remainder of butter cream in center. Sprinkle with trimmings from top layer.

To make rum cream filling: Whip cream until stiff. Beat in rum and sugar. Spread whipped cream over buttercream on bottom layer. Place decorated meringue on top and refrigerate.

Florentines

YIELDS 6 DOZEN 2-INCH COOKIES

6   tablespoons butter
¾   cup whipping cream
3   cups sliced almonds
½   cup finely chopped candied orange peel
⅔   cup thinly sliced candied cherries
1   cup plus 2 tablespoons sugar
½   teaspoon vanilla extract (see p. 254)
¾   cup plus 2 tablespoons flour
¼   teaspoon ground cinnamon
⅛   teaspoon salt
5   ounces semisweet chocolate

Preheat oven to 325°.

In heavy saucepan, bring butter and cream to boiling point over medium heat. Add almonds, candied fruits, sugar, vanilla extract, flour, cinnamon, and salt. Stir well; cook about 5 minutes. Turn heat to very low to keep batter warm.

Grease and flour several cookie sheets. Drop mixture by teaspoonfuls about 3 inches apart, flattening slightly. Bake 12 to 15 minutes or until golden brown. Remove from sheets and cool on rack.

Melt chocolate over warm, *not boiling*, water. Stir to smooth consistency. Do not heat chocolate over 100° (90° ideal temperature for glazing wafers). Coat bottom of each wafer. Let chocolate harden completely before serving or storing.

Ginger Cookies

YIELDS ABOUT 6 DOZEN 2-INCH COOKIES

¾   cup butter
1   cup sugar
1   egg
4   tablespoons molasses
½   teaspoon salt
½   teaspoon ground cinnamon
½   teaspoon ground ginger
½   teaspoon ground cloves
2   teaspoons baking soda
2½   cups flour

Melt butter over low heat. Remove from heat and cool. Add sugar, egg, and molasses; beat well.

Sift together salt, spices, baking soda, and flour. Add to egg mixture; mix well. Shape into 2 rolls about 1 inch in diameter; wrap in waxed paper. Chill overnight or freeze. Dough is soft.

Preheat oven to 325°.

Slice rolls into rounds about ⅛ inch thick. Place on greased cookie sheet about 1 inch apart. Bake 10 to 12 minutes. Cool on racks. Cookies should be very crisp.

Apple Strudel

YIELDS 8 PASTRIES

Filling:

12	large apples, peeled, cored, and very thinly sliced
1	cup ground almonds
1	cup currants
1	cup sugar
2	teaspoons ground cinnamon
¼	teaspoon ground cardamom
1	teaspoon grated lemon zest

Wrapping:

1	pound filo leaves (14 × 10 inches, 24 leaves)
1	pound butter, melted
½	pound fresh bread crumbs

Powdered sugar

Preheat oven to 450°.

Have on hand a large working space, several baking sheets, dampened tea towels or pastry cloths, pastry brush, and foil for freezing. (Also, if making for the first time or working slowly, a water spray. Plant mister will suffice.)

Combine all filling ingredients in very large bowl. Stir together with wooden spoon. Set aside until juice begins to form. Stir occasionally while wrapping pastry to keep all ingredients evenly distributed.

To assemble strudel: Layer work surface in overlapped tea towels. Spread single layer of filo leaf on damp surface. Quickly brush leaf with butter. Sprinkle with 1 or 2 table-spoons bread crumbs. (Repeat with second and then third filo leaf.) Place 1½ cups filling along one long end. Using tea towels, coax strudel into long roll, being careful not to lose too much filling out the sides. Continue to roll until complete. Transfer to baking sheet, using towels. Tuck ends under. Brush with butter; top with crumbs. Continue until all ingredients are used.

Bake 10 minutes. Lower temperature to 400° and bake additional 20 minutes until pastry is pale golden in color and quite crisp. Dust with powdered sugar; serve at once.

Water spray is used if dough begins to dry out. If work is done quickly, spray will not be necessary. Strudel freezes very well. Roll in foil. Seal well; freeze before baking.

Grandmother's Buttermilk Cake

SERVES 12 TO 14

1	cup shortening
3	cups sugar
4	eggs
3	cups flour
½	teaspoon baking soda
¼	teaspoon salt
1	cup buttermilk
1	teaspoon vanilla extract (see p. 224)
2	teaspoons lemon extract
¼	teaspoon ground mace

Preheat oven to 350°.

Cream shortening and sugar. Add eggs, one at a time, beating well after each addition.

Sift together flour, baking soda, and salt; add to mixture alternately with buttermilk. Add vanilla and lemon extracts and mace; mix well.

Butter and sugar 9¼-inch tube pan. Pour batter into pan and bake approximately 1 hour. Cool in pan 15 to 20 minutes. Turn out onto cake rack with top side up to finish cooling.

Chocolate Bavarian Dessert Cake

SERVES 14 TO 16

3   4-ounce packages German sweet
     chocolate
6   eggs, separated
3   tablespoons sugar
1   cup chopped pecans
1½   cups whipping cream
1   sponge cake
Whipped cream (optional)

Sponge Cake:
1½   cups cake flour, sifted *before* measuring
1½   cups sugar, divided
½   teaspoon baking powder
½   teaspoon salt
5   eggs, separated
1½   teaspoons vanilla extract (see p. 224)
½   cup cold water
¾   teaspoon cream of tartar

Preheat oven to 325°.
Sift together 5 times already-sifted flour, 1 cup sugar, baking powder, and salt. Set aside.
Beat egg yolks until lemon colored. Add ½ cup sugar; beat until thick. Set aside.
Combine vanilla extract and water. Stir into egg yolks alternately with flour mixture.
Beat egg whites and cream of tartar until stiff but not dry. Fold into batter carefully. Pour batter into ungreased 10-inch tube pan; bake 50 to 60 minutes. Remove from oven and cool upside down about 5 minutes, inserting bottle or funnel into tube to hold pan above table surface. Run knife around edges to loosen cake. Turn out on rack to continue to cool.

To assemble cake: Melt chocolate in top of double boiler. Add well-beaten egg yolks and sugar. Cook until thickened, stirring constantly. Remove from heat; beat until cooled. Add pecans.
Beat cream until it holds peaks; fold into chocolate mixture.
Beat egg whites until stiff; fold into chocolate mixture.
Line 10-cup (10½ × 3 inch) ring mold with waxed paper. Pour in small amount of chocolate mixture barely covering bottom. Cut cake horizontally into ½-inch slices. Place 1 slice on top of chocolate. Continue filling mold, alternating slices of cake and chocolate. Cover mold with plastic wrap; refrigerate overnight.
Invert on serving platter; remove mold and waxed paper. Fill center with whipped cream if desired.

French Nut Roll

SERVES 8

6   eggs, separated
1   cup sugar
1   cup finely chopped pecans
2   teaspoons baking powder
1   cup whipped cream
3   tablespoons rum
Powdered sugar

Preheat oven to 350°.
Beat egg yolks, add sugar and beat until mixture becomes pale and thickened. Add pecans.
Beat egg whites until foamy. Add baking powder and beat until stiff. Fold into yolk mixture.
Oil 11 × 16–inch jelly roll pan; line with waxed paper and oil waxed paper. Spread mixture onto pan; bake 20 minutes. Immediately cover cake with damp cloth until it has cooled. Put into refrigerator until ready to assemble.
Turn out onto towel powdered with sugar. Peel off waxed paper. Spread with whipped cream flavored with rum and roll up. Sprinkle with more powdered sugar if desired.

Irish Whiskey Cake

SERVES 16

Cake:
½   pound butter, softened
2   cups sugar
6   eggs
4   cups cake flour
2   teaspoons baking powder
2   teaspoons grated nutmeg
½   teaspoon salt
1   teaspoon vanilla extract (see p. 224)
1   cup Irish whiskey
2   cups pecan halves

Sauce:
4   tablespoons butter, softened
1¼ cups sifted powdered sugar
2   eggs, separated
⅛   teaspoon salt
½   teaspoon grated nutmeg
¼   cup Irish whiskey
½   cup whipping cream

Preheat oven to 300°.
Cream butter and sugar until light and fluffy. Add eggs one at a time, beating after each addition. Mix well.
Sift together flour, baking powder, nutmeg, and salt. Add vanilla extract and whiskey alternately with dry ingredients to batter. Stir in pecan halves.
Bake in 10-inch greased angel food cake pan 2½ hours. Place pan of water in oven while baking. Cool 10 to 15 minutes in pan. Turn out onto rack.

To make sauce: Beat butter and sugar together.
Beat egg yolks and salt. In double boiler over simmering water, beat egg yolks into butter-sugar mixture, stirring constantly until mixture has thickened. Remove from heat. Stir in nutmeg and whiskey; chill 2 to 4 hours.
Beat egg whites until soft peaks form. Fold into custard. Whip cream; fold in before serving.

Quick Amaretto Ice Cream

YIELDS 2 QUARTS

2   cups sugar
2   cups Amaretto
8   egg yolks
1   quart whipping cream

In 2-quart saucepan, heat sugar and Amaretto until thick and syrupy. Set aside.

In large bowl, beat egg yolks until light and lemon colored. Pour sugar mixture very slowly into egg yolks, beating constantly until thick. Cool.

Whip cream until peaks form. Fold whipped cream into egg mixture. Blend well. Place in container; cover tightly and freeze.

Praline Ice Cream Sauce

YIELDS 2½ CUPS

⅓   cup boiling water
⅓   cup brown sugar
1   cup white corn syrup
1   cup chopped pecans
3   tablespoons praline liqueur or brandy

Add sugar to water; bring back to boil. Add corn syrup. Return to boil and cook 1 minute, stirring constantly. Remove from heat. Cool slightly. Add pecans and liqueur. Refrigerate. Mixture will thicken when cold.

Strawberry Bouquets

SERVES 4

1   pint strawberries
1   kiwi fruit
4   tablespoons crème de menthe

Have all ingredients chilled before assembling.

Clean berries and arrange in 4 crystal serving dishes.

Peel and slice kiwi fruit. Arrange green slices around red berries as "leaves." Spoon 1 tablespoon crème de menthe over each serving.

Sauce Sabayon à l'Orange

YIELDS 3 TO 3½ CUPS

6   egg yolks
6   tablespoons sugar
6   tablespoons orange-flavored liqueur, divided
1   cup whipping cream

Place egg yolks, sugar, and 4 tablespoons liqueur into round-bottomed china or stainless steel bowl. Place bowl over pan of barely simmering water and cook, beating constantly with whisk or electric beater, until mixture is very thick. Remove from heat and cool.

Whip cream until stiff. Fold into egg mixture with remaining liqueur. Serve over fresh raspberries, peaches, strawberries, and so on.

Peanut Butter Cups

YIELDS 3½ TO 4 DOZEN

**4 to 5 ounces 100% natural peanut butter
    (i.e., no added salt or sugar)**
3   tablespoons butter
¾   cup powdered sugar
½   teaspoon salt
4 to 6 ounces semisweet chocolate, melted
Small paper candy holders (optional)

Mix together peanut butter, butter, powdered sugar, and salt until smooth and creamy. Form into 2 rolls, about 1 inch in diameter. Wrap in waxed paper. Chill overnight.

Slice into rounds about ⅜ inch thick. Dip pieces into chocolate, covering only one-half or completely. Place on waxed paper to let chocolate set. If desired, place peanut butter round in paper candy holder; then spread melted chocolate over top of piece.

Caramels

MAKES 3 TO 4 DOZEN 1-INCH PIECES

½   cup sugar
½   cup light brown sugar
¼   teaspoon salt
½   cup dark corn syrup
¼   pound butter
1   cup whipping cream, divided
½   pound pecan halves
½   tablespoon vanilla extract (see p. 224)

Mix sugars, salt, syrup, butter, and ½ cup cream in heavy 3- to 4-quart pot. Bring to boil over medium-high heat. Add remaining cream slowly so mixture keeps boiling. Reduce heat to medium, but keep mixture boiling. Cook until temperature reaches 240° on candy thermometer, stirring occasionally to keep from burning. This will take 20 to 25 minutes.

Remove from heat, add pecans and vanilla extract. Mix well. Spread on buttered cookie sheets with sides. Chill. Cut into squares. May be served plain or dipped in chocolate.

CONTRIBUTORS

The success of a work like the *Houston Fine Arts Cookbook* depends on the energies and enthusiasm of hundreds of people who give their cherished recipes, culinary talents, and hours of typing, cross-referencing, and proofreading and, most of all, sacrifice their svelte waistlines in the line of duty. As editor it has been my great privilege to work closely with a number of these dedicated volunteers during the past two years. They are a grand and inspiring group to whom I give special thanks.

—Virginia T. Elverson, Editor

General Chair: Susie Morris

Committee Chairs:

Lainey Abbott	Maxine Davis	Sarah McMurrey	Marilyn Tesoro
Holly Anderson	Linda Fosseen	Cinda Matthews	Ellen Wilkerson
Carole Boyd	Nancy Goodrich	Susie Morris	
Beverly Brannan	Ann Hamilton	Edith Pearson	
Polly Daniel	Joan Loveland	Shirley Shockley	

Behind-the-Scenes:

Celeste Adams	Polly Daniel	Joan Loveland	Deborah Roberts
Marilyn Allen	Beth Fine	Margie Lynch	Susan Sinks
Sally Avery	Lainie Fink	Judith McCandless	Margaret Skidmore
Karen Battelstein	Donna Fleming	Virginia McKallip	Georgia Stacy
Carole Boyd	Charlotte Fox	Sarah McMurrey	Marilyn Tesoro
Ronnie Boyd	Nancy Goodrich	Edward Mayo	Anne Tucker
Beverly Brannan	Katherine Howe	Marty Moore	Virginia Walker
Michael Brown	Anne Hysell	Ann Naber	Ellen Wilkerson
Anne Bushman	Marilyn Kurk	Maggie Olvey	Helen Worley
Dorwayne Clemens	Mary Gray Lester	Edith Pearson	
Darla Comeaux	Linda Letzerich	Kimberly Powell	

Test Cooks:

Lainey Abbott	Sarah Bergner	Catherine Clagge	Gale Davis
Holly Anderson	Pauline Bolton	Lollie Cluett	Maxine Davis
Page Andrew	Carole Boyd	Darla Comeaux	Mercedes Dewey
Patsy Arcidiacono	Judy Brand	Alida Coogan	Ellen Donnelly
Sally Avery	Beverly Brannan	Nancy Cope	Margo Downey
Dorothy Baird	Pam Briggs	Donna Crawford	Beth Fine
Bonnie Barnes	Ann Brinkerhoff	Claire Cullinan	Lainie Fink
Cynthia Baskin	Joey Buck	Betty Current	Linda Fosseen
Karen Battelstein	Anne Bushman	Nancy Damon	Charlotte Fox
Betty Bellamy	Jean-Marie Church	Polly Daniel	Teri Friedman

Carlys Hudgins
Mrs. John Huebner, Jr.
Mickie Huebsch
Ann Huggins
Martha Hunter
Anne Hysell
Barbara Jackson
Mrs. Lewis Johnson
Jo Jones
Petie Jonsson
Madeline Judkins
Betty C. Jukes
Ginger Kanaly
Jean Kaufman
Freya Keefe
Martha Kelley
Patricia F. Kent
Kay King
Katie Kitchen
Jean Klein
Mrs. Philip C. Koelsch
Connie Koomey
Laurie Krueger
Marilyn Kurk
Elizabeth Lancaster
Mary Anne Larsen
Jeanne Lasher
Midge Lassiter
Nancy Lazarus
Alicia Lee
Ann Lents
Mary Gray Lester
Mrs. Robert Ligon
Cecilia Lind
Betty Lipson
Mrs. John R. Lively

Joan Loveland
Mrs. Albert S. Low
Oveta S. Lucy
Mrs. A. D. Lundstedt
Helen McArdle
Barbara Lee McCall
Florence McCarville
Marie L. McCormick
Mrs. S. E. McCormick
Adrienne McCullough
Donna McDowell
Virginia McFarland
Jessie McGaio
Jessie B. McGaw
Stevie Mackie
Ann Maloney
Barbara Manley
Wendy Mars
Caroll Masterson
Harris Masterson
Betty Mendell
Ruthee Meric
Mrs. Richard Merrill
Joyce Meyers
Ted Miller
Edwina Milner
Ellen A. Molish
Betty Kyle Moore
Carolyn B. Moore
Jeanne Moore
Sandy Morgan
William S. Myers
Ann Naber
Catherine Newman
Phyllis Nold
Susan Oaks

Clarice Marik O'Hare
Ann O'Malley
Katie Oliver
Larry Olson
Hanni Orton
Barbara Owsley
Rose Pan
Rose Paolucci
Gwendolyn Pappas
Mrs. Walter L. Parsley
Mary Jean Pawley
Judy Prim
Janie Raine
Caroll Reiff
G. Phil Roberts
Michele Roberts
Sally Roberts
Karen Robinson
Jane Root
Rae Royle
Virginia Russell
Karen Sanchez
Jeanne Sanders
Mrs. Fayez Sarofim
Jacqueline Schmeal
Petty Schoelman
Idell Scrivner
Richard Seinfeld
Martha Ann Selzman
Sue Seymour
Sigrid Shakno
Mildred Sherwood
Shirley Shockley
Mrs. Willard Shuart
Micki Simms
Mrs. Lomis Slaughter

Minnie Mae Spears
Wells Stewart
Patsy Strand
Helen Sullivan
Nancy Terry
Marilyn Tesoro
Dana Thacker
Eleanor Tinsley
Sally Tonelli
Ann Trammell
Patricia Trumble
Katherine Tyson
Carolyn Vance
Joan Vaseliades
Suneeta Vaswani
Terry Vekris
Janet Waldherr
Ricka Waldron
Gailee Walker
Katherine Walker
Virginia Walker
Julia Wallace
Bettie Wallingford
Mrs. Peter Whiteford
Susan Whitehead
Ellen Wilkerson
Earline Willcott
Betty Williams
Frances Williams
Lou Ellen Wooten
Haskell Wotkyns, Jr.
Gertrude Yang
Maggie Zimmer
Fran Zomper